Developing Global Professionals for the U.S. Federal Workforce

Insights from the Careers of Boren Scholarship and Fellowship Awards Alumni

JENNIFER J. LI, LISA WAGNER, RICHARD S. GIRVEN, STEPHEN LEE, SHREYA S. HUILGOL, DENIS AGNIEL

Prepared for the Office of the Secretary of Defense
Approved for public release; distribution is unlimited

RAND NATIONAL DEFENSE RESEARCH INSTITUTE

For more information on this publication, visit **www.rand.org/t/RRA494-1**.

About RAND

The RAND Corporation is a research organization that develops solutions to public policy challenges to help make communities throughout the world safer and more secure, healthier and more prosperous. RAND is nonprofit, nonpartisan, and committed to the public interest. To learn more about RAND, visit www.rand.org.

Research Integrity

Our mission to help improve policy and decisionmaking through research and analysis is enabled through our core values of quality and objectivity and our unwavering commitment to the highest level of integrity and ethical behavior. To help ensure our research and analysis are rigorous, objective, and nonpartisan, we subject our research publications to a robust and exacting quality-assurance process; avoid both the appearance and reality of financial and other conflicts of interest through staff training, project screening, and a policy of mandatory disclosure; and pursue transparency in our research engagements through our commitment to the open publication of our research findings and recommendations, disclosure of the source of funding of published research, and policies to ensure intellectual independence. For more information, visit www.rand.org/about/principles.

RAND's publications do not necessarily reflect the opinions of its research clients and sponsors.

Published by the RAND Corporation, Santa Monica, Calif.
© 2024 RAND Corporation
RAND® is a registered trademark.

Library of Congress Cataloging-in-Publication Data is available for this publication.
ISBN: 978-1-9774-1-3949

About This Report

International skills—including foreign-language capabilities, cultural knowledge, and regional expertise—are critical to the U.S. government workforce and national security. To help meet that need, the David L. Boren National Security Education Act of 1991 (Public Law 102-183; 105 Stat. 1271; approved December 4, 1991) established the Boren Scholarship and Fellowship Awards program. The Boren Awards provide funding for long-term, overseas, immersive study to U.S. undergraduate and graduate students who are committed to public service. This report provides findings and recommendations from research on the Boren Awards program to help evaluate the program's outcomes and inform its ongoing efforts to build and sustain a federal workforce of diverse language- and culture-enabled individuals. It may also be of interest to others seeking to strengthen the talent pipeline to the federal workforce. The research reported here was completed in January 2024 and underwent security review with the sponsor and the Defense Office of Prepublication and Security Review before public release.

RAND National Security Research Division

This research was sponsored by the Office of the Under Secretary of Defense for Personnel and Readiness and the Defense Human Resources Activity, with the Defense Language and National Security Education Office. It was conducted within the Personnel, Readiness, and Health Program of the RAND National Security Research Division (NSRD), which operates the National Defense Research Institute (NDRI), a federally funded research and development center sponsored by the Office of the Secretary of Defense, the Joint Staff, the Unified Combatant Commands, the Navy, the Marine Corps, the defense agencies, and the defense intelligence enterprise.

For more information on the RAND Personnel, Readiness, and Health Program, see www.rand.org/nsrd/prh or contact the director (contact information is provided on the webpage).

Acknowledgments

We are grateful to Shawn G. Skelly, performing the duties of Deputy Under Secretary of Defense for Personnel and Readiness; Jeffrey R. Register, director, Defense Human Resources Activity; and M. Alex Baird, director, Defense Support Services Center, for supporting this work.

We thank the leadership team and staff at the Defense Language and National Security Education Office and the National Security Education Program for their collegiality and assistance throughout this effort—specifically, Samuel Eisen, Alison Patz, Clare Bugary, Ed McDermott, Mariah Stewart, and Caitlin Wiley. We appreciate the engagement from William Booth, Thomas Constable, and Michael Nugent, who facilitated this research while in their previous positions.

We thank Molly McIntosh for her support of this project. Finally, many thanks go to Lindsay Daugherty, Daniel Ginsberg, and Hugh MacFarlane for their valuable review feedback and suggestions.

Summary

Following two world wars and the Cold War, U.S. defense and national security policies have increasingly recognized the importance of foreign language capabilities, cultural skills, and regional expertise related to U.S. allies and adversaries alike. However, these capabilities—especially foreign language and cultural skills—have been consistently underrepresented in the federal workforce. The David L. Boren National Security Education Act of 1991 (Public Law 102-183, 105 Stat. 1271, as amended) took significant, enduring steps to address this critical shortage. One of the Boren Act's provisions authorized the Boren Scholarship and Fellowship Awards, which award funding for long-term, overseas, immersive study to U.S. undergraduate and graduate students who are committed to public service. Boren awardees study less commonly taught languages while living in cultures and countries less commonly chosen by U.S. students. In doing so, they acquire language and global skills critical to U.S. national security while attaining their undergraduate or graduate degrees. In exchange, they agree to use the skills within the U.S. Department of Defense (DoD) or other federal agencies by working in the federal government for at least one year after graduating.

Issue

The Boren Awards program was last evaluated in 2014 when the Defense Language and National Security Education Office (DLNSEO) engaged CNA to survey Boren alumni to determine how the program had affected the careers of those who had received Boren Awards from the program's inception in 1991 through 2012. Since the 2014 survey, more than 2,000 new Boren awardees have completed the federal employment service commitment, yielding an alumni count of more than 4,600. The Office of the Under Secretary of Defense for Personnel and Readiness, Defense Human Resources Activity, and DLNSEO asked the RAND National Defense Research Institute to conduct a new survey to learn about the career paths and career decisions of Boren awardees from 1994 to early 2023, understand how policy changes since 2013 may have affected awardees' experiences, and inform plans to strengthen the program in the future.

Approach

The RAND team design a mixed methods approach to examine the program and Boren awardees' careers. The research centered on a web-based survey combined with stakeholder discussions and a literature review to address the following research questions:

- What career paths have Boren alumni taken after completing their degree programs?
- What do Boren alumni report as the strongest influences on their career choices, whether they stayed in government service or transitioned to the private sector?

- What factors facilitate or impede the employment of Boren alumni in DoD and other federal agencies?
- What program improvements would enable Boren alumni to use the skills and experience acquired through the Boren program more fully in service to DoD and other federal agencies?

Key Findings

Workforce and Worker Trends

Regarding worker and workforce trends, we found the following:

- Workforce trends showing waning interest in federal jobs attest to the value of programs like Boren that attract and prepare early-career talent to join the federal national security workforce.
- However, generational differences may call for program adjustments to better meet the needs of the present and future cohorts of new workers.

Boren Alumni Experiences and Careers

In relation to alumni experiences and careers, we found the following:

- In our survey, most alumni reported positive experiences with the Boren program and described it as very significant to their career success.
- Even though most alumni completed the Boren service requirement smoothly, some reported difficulties and suggested that more support and flexibility be provided.
- Consistent with the program's purpose to bring globally enabled talent to the federal national security workforce, the most common employment sector for Boren awardees in their first, second, and third positions after graduating was the federal government.
- On average, Boren awardees tended to stay substantially longer in jobs that satisfied their service requirements, even though their federal service was completed after one year.
- Boren alumni spoke highly about the quality of the program, but some were disappointed that some federal employers were unaware of the Boren program.

Facilitators and Impediments to Federal Employment for Boren Alumni

Regarding factors that affected awardees' ability to secure federal employment for alumni, we found the following:

- Some respondents reported that the Boren special hiring authorities facilitated their employment in DoD and other federal agencies.

- The factors they reported as hindering federal employment included difficulty finding qualifying positions that matched their skills, the Boren program's lack of widespread name recognition among employers, a lack of awareness and understanding of special hiring authorities by some federal employers, and a need for more personalized support for those who have difficulty securing qualifying federal employment.

Recommendations

Based on our findings, we recommend the following:

- Expand and increase the supports available to Boren awardees who face difficulties while seeking employment to fulfill their federal service requirements.
- Adopt a business-strategic approach to clearly identify the key stakeholder groups that are important to the continued growth and success of the Boren program, and then engage with each audience in ways more tailored to its needs.
- Build values of diversity, equity, and inclusion into Boren practices—especially in relation to outreach, communication, award selection, awardee supports, and community building.
- Invigorate and grow the Boren community around a compelling shared ethos—for example, by articulating a set of values and professional characteristics that Boren community members support, promote, and share—and then use these values and characteristics as the foundation for the Boren brand in program decisions and internal and external communications.[1]

---

[1] We use the term *ethos* to mean "the characteristic spirit of a culture, era, or community as manifested in its beliefs and aspirations" (Oxford Dictionaries Online, undated). This ties directly to our recommendation that NSEP work to clearly define and market the features of the Boren program that make it distinct and special, such as mission, values, ethos, and the value proposition that should make Boren alumni stand out among other programs.

Contents

Figures and Tables

Figures

Tables

CHAPTER 1

Introduction and Overview of the Boren Awards

Following two world wars and the Cold War, U.S. defense and national security policies have increasingly recognized the importance of international capabilities, specifically foreign language skills, cultural knowledge, and regional expertise. At a time when the United States worried about losing its competitive edge to the Soviet Union, the National Defense Education Act (NDEA) of 1958 (P.L. 85-864, 72 Stat. 150; approved September 2, 1958) was the first legislation to provide federal funding for education (starting with mathematics, science, and modern foreign languages) in the interest of national security. The scarcity of foreign language skills among U.S. citizens continued to concern policymakers through the 1970s and 1980s—as evidenced, for example, by President Jimmy Carter's Commission on Foreign Language and International Studies in the 1970s and the publication of then-representative Paul Simon's *The Tongue-Tied American* in 1980.

The persistent shortage of foreign language capabilities and other international skills in the federal workforce was serious enough to lead to further federal legislation: the David L. Boren National Security Education Act (NSEA) of 1991 (Public Law 102-183, 105 Stat. 1271, as amended) took significant, enduring steps to address the critical shortage.

The Boren Act authorized the Boren Scholarship and Fellowship Awards, which award funding for long-term, overseas, immersive study to U.S. undergraduate and graduate students committed to public service. Boren awardees study less commonly taught languages while living among cultures and in countries less commonly chosen by U.S. students. In doing so, they acquire language and global skills critical to U.S. national security while attaining their undergraduate or graduate degrees. In exchange, they agree to use those skills in the federal government by working for one year in the U.S. Department of Defense (DoD), the U.S. Department of Homeland Security (DHS), the U.S. Department of State (DOS), or in the U.S. intelligence community (or another federal agency with national security responsibilities) after they graduate. Since their inception, the Boren Awards have funded thousands of undergraduate and graduate students to study 124 languages in 130 countries. As of 2023, more than 4,600 of them have fulfilled their federal service requirements by working in federally funded positions contributing to national security or have begun to do so (Defense Language and National Security Education Office [DLNSEO], 2023).

Defense Human Resources Activity, DLNSEO, and the Office of the Under Secretary of Defense for Personnel and Readiness asked the RAND National Defense Research Institute to evaluate the Boren Scholarship and Fellowship Awards program to understand how it has affected awardees' careers and to recommend ways to strengthen it where appropriate. This report shares the findings of our research. These findings may also be of interest to other agencies seeking to broaden and strengthen the talent pool for federal service.

Federal Workforce and Generational Trends as a Backdrop to the Boren Program

Workforce and generational trends affect federal recruiting overall, as well as the Boren program because of its role in bringing specialized talent to the federal workforce.

Recent statistics on federal workers make educating, preparing, and attracting the future federal workforce more important now than ever. The federal workforce is growing older on average (White House, 2022), and retention of younger workers is low (Jones, 2020). Employees under the age of 30 represent nearly one-fourth of the U.S. *total* workforce, but only less than 10 percent of the U.S. *federal* workforce (White House, 2022). Negative perceptions about government employment, regarding pay freezes, shutdowns, bureaucracy (Rose, 2012; Viechnicki, 2015), and lack of innovation (Santinha et al., 2021) may steer public-service-oriented individuals to nonprofit, nongovernmental, or social entrepreneurship opportunities instead. Meanwhile, the need for government workers with foreign language skills continues to grow (McGinn, 2014; Rose, 2012).

The generation of individuals currently entering the workforce—Gen Z, born between 1997 and 2010—has some traits worth noting, which also came up in the survey data. Gen Z individuals are more likely to enter the adult workforce without prior work experience as teens (Schroth, 2019). As a group, Gen Z embodies more diversity than any previous generation (Pew Research Center, 2018; and diversity, equity, and inclusion are more important to them than to any other generation (Deloitte, 2023; Twenge, 2017). Gen Z individuals report high levels of stress and anxiety, and they tend to value resources and policies that support mental health in their workplaces (Deloitte, 2023). They also value flexibility (Deloitte, 2023).

Even though these trends suggest a need for strong, updated approaches to federal recruiting, the Boren program has some immutable advantages. First, government experience is a strong predictor for continued interest in government careers (Bright, 2018; Bright and Graham, 2015; Partnership for Public Service/National Association of Colleges and Employers, 2012), and programs like the Boren Awards provide crucial exposure to government jobs while individuals are choosing careers. Second, people motivated to serve the public have higher levels of job satisfaction when doing work that contributes to society (Homberg, McCarthy, and Tabvuma, 2015); thus, the Boren program, which selects only public-service-motivated individuals, gives its awardees a pathway to jobs they may more likely find satisfying.

Boren Awards Program Overview

The Boren Act's five interrelated purposes underpin every aspect of its scholarship and fellowship awards program:

(1) To provide the necessary resources, accountability, and flexibility to meet the national security education needs of the United States, especially as such needs change over time.

(2) To increase the quantity, diversity, and quality of the teaching and learning of subjects in the fields of foreign languages, area studies, counterproliferation studies, and other international fields that are critical to the Nation's interest.

(3) To produce an increased pool of applicants for work in the departments and agencies of the United States Government with national security responsibilities.

(4) To expand, in conjunction with other Federal programs, the international experience, knowledge base, and perspectives on which the United States citizenry, Government employees, and leaders rely.

(5) To permit the Federal Government to advocate the cause of international education. (Public Law 102-183, 105 Stat. 1271, as amended)

By design, the Boren Awards seek applicants who demonstrate a longer-term commitment to government service (Boren Awards, undated-b). The program provides prospective applicants with a list of preferred languages, countries, and fields of study (Boren Awards, undated-c). The award amounts vary based on study abroad duration, with preference given to applicants proposing overseas programs of at least 25 weeks (Boren Awards, undated-d). The award to a Boren Scholar (undergraduate student) or Fellow (graduate student) who plans to study abroad for between 12 and 24 weeks is $12,500. For study abroad for 25 to 52 weeks, the award is $25,000 (Boren Awards, undated-c). In 2022, more than 75 percent of Boren awardees planned to study abroad for an entire academic year.

In 1994, the first cohort of students received their awards. The 317 scholarship and 172 fellowship awardees represented more than 150 U.S. higher education institutions. They studied more than 50 different languages in nearly 60 countries, with awards ranging from $1,000 to $30,000 each.

As context for the research discussion to come, the following sections of this chapter give an overview of the Boren Awards program and its evolution in terms of the key factors that shape its implementation and outcomes: the program offering, the federal service requirement established in 1996, the administrative and support services, and the Boren network and community. The following sections describe each of these factors.

Boren Awards Give Students Access to a Wide Range of Intensive Language-Learning Opportunities

The Boren Awards fund rigorous, intensive language study in Africa, Asia, central and eastern Europe, Latin America, and the Middle East to study languages critical to national security in strategic regions where U.S. students have been underrepresented. It explicitly does *not* fund study to Australia, Canada, western Europe, and New Zealand, countries in which U.S. students are well represented. From 1994 through 2010, all eligible students designed their own bespoke intensive language study programs within set criteria for language, country, field of study, and program duration. The scope and flexibility of Boren learning options may have made the program highly desirable for many and yet potentially daunting for those seeking to learn some of the least commonly taught critical languages in countries less frequented by U.S. students.

In the following decade, the National Security Education Program (NSEP) added new regional programs, with preselected language learning programs offering domestic summer language study followed by language study overseas for the fall semester and, optionally, the following spring. The first was the African Flagship Languages Initiative, which provides intensive study in any of five African languages: Akwan/Twi, French, Swahili, Wolof, and Zulu. Next, the South Asian Flagship Languages Initiative launched in 2016 for Hindi and Urdu. In 2017, NSEP added the Indonesian Flagship Languages Initiative for Indonesian. This was followed in 2019 by the Turkish Flagship Language Initiative for Turkish. Starting in 2024, NSEP will combine Indonesian, Thai, and Vietnamese into the Southeast Asian Languages Flagship Initiative. Being able to design their own programs or learn through a regional Flagship initiative gives students access to a wide range of languages, cultures, and regions they might not otherwise be able to experience.

The Language Flagship program supports undergraduate students of all majors in their pursuit of professional language proficiency in a critical language at their home universities. Students who qualify with advanced language proficiency are eligible for the Language Flagship overseas capstone programs, which include an academic year in-country with intensive language study, direct enrollment in local university courses related to their fields of study, and professional internships. Language Flagship students may apply for the Boren Flagship Scholarship to support their overseas studies. There are a growing number of Language Flagship students receiving Boren Flagship Scholarships to pursue their intensive overseas capstone programs in Arabic, Chinese, Korean, Portuguese, and Russian.

The Boren Service Requirement Brings Awardees' Foreign-Language and International Skills to Federal Agencies

When a Boren awardee completes their overseas studies and undergraduate or graduate degree, they are expected to bring those international skills—language proficiency, cultural knowledge, and regional expertise—to a job with national security responsibilities in the federal workforce for a year. If an appropriate federal job is unavailable, the awardee may instead work in a higher education position that uses the field of study, language, or regional expertise for which they received the award. If they do not at least begin a job that will meet the service requirement (via either option)—within three years for a Scholar or two years for a Fellow—the awardee must repay part of the award, with interest set by DoD.

The Boren service requirements have changed in important ways since the first Boren Awards were given in 1994. We describe relevant changes here in some detail for context because awardees' experiences with the service requirement may color their views of the overall program, which we will discuss later. In the early years of the program, some awardees struggled to secure jobs that would fulfill their service requirements. Nearly every update of the service requirement since then expanded the range of options to fulfill it. In addition, the special hiring authorities introduced in 2009 arguably made the Boren service requirement less of an obligation and more of a federal career opportunity by offering a noncompetitive fast track to career-status (rather than temporary) positions. Appendix A provides a detailed timeline of these changes to the service requirement and other key program updates over time.

Starting in 1996, the Boren legislation required each Boren Scholar (undergraduate student) who studied abroad for 12 months or longer to work in federal service for a period *not longer than* the length of the funded study abroad. Each Boren Fellow (graduate student) who studied abroad 12 months or longer was expected to work in federal service for *at least the same duration* as the funded study abroad. These terms changed in 1996 when the legislation was updated to apply the same length requirement to both Scholars and Fellows. It set the length of the service requirement to be equal to the duration of the awardee's study abroad. That policy remained through 2004.

In 2005, the U.S. Congress updated the service-requirement legislation, making the Boren service requirement equal to 12 months or longer, depending on the length of an awardee's study abroad. Further, only two areas of government were eligible: DoD and the intelligence community. By 2008, the legislation was amended to expand the options to complete the service requirement. Government service could be in DHS, DoD, the DOS (including its work with the U.S. Agency for International Development [USAID]), and the intelligence community. Alternatively, it could be in other federal positions with national security responsibilities or in an education position related to the language, region, or topic studied with Boren funding. It also provided an option to waive the service requirement in cases of extreme hardship, medical disability, security clearance denial, and hiring freezes.

In late 2009, the National Defense Authorization Act (NDAA) for fiscal year (FY) 2010 (Public Law 111-84, Sec. 1101), further amended the Boren Act legislation with special hiring authorities that allowed federal agencies to hire Boren Scholars and Fellows with not-yet-fulfilled service requirements through noncompetitive appointments. And if a Boren awardee hired under the authorities reached two years of satisfactory service, their federal employer could convert them from temporary or term employee to career or career-conditional status, again without competition. In 2013, those special hiring authorities were expanded to allow federal agencies to appoint Boren awardees noncompetitively to career or career-conditional positions, regardless of Boren service-requirement completion. These changes were designed to make Boren hiring easier, faster, and more attractive for federal employers, to expand job opportunities for Boren awardees, and, ultimately, to create conditions that would draw globally enabled talent to long-term careers with national security responsibilities in the federal government.

Administrative and Support Services Affect Awardees' Experiences

For interested students, applicants, awardees, and alumni, the management, administration, and support services that keep the program running are critically important.

In 1994, the Boren Scholarship Awards were administered by the nonprofit Institute of International Education (IIE). The Fellowship Awards were administered by a separate non-profit, the Academy for Educational Development. In 2006, the administrative operations for both award programs were consolidated to IIE. IIE serves as NSEP's administrative agent, collaborating closely with NSEP, and while IIE takes the lead on outreach to the NSEP application population, administering the application process and providing support services to Scholars and Fellows before and during study abroad, all aspects of program management after awardees' return from overseas is managed exclusively by NSEP. This includes not only management of the service requirement but also strategically planning and executing outreach to federal hiring managers and supporting the active job-seeking population via a variety of mechanisms (e.g., individualized résumé and cover letter reviews, job application reviews, mock interviews, the Boren mentorship program, job fairs, an annual federal employment seminar, exclusive job listings, and other job search resources).

In the program's early years, support services for Boren awardees before, during, and after study abroad were limited, but they have grown over time. They now include résumé, cover letter, and job application review; mock interviews; the Boren mentorship program; a federal employment seminar; exclusive job listings; and other job search assistance, among other resources (NSEP, undated-b; NSEP, undated-d). The job portal NSEP-NET was created to help Boren job seekers find federal job opportunities and to enable federal employers to share job openings with Boren alumni. In 2001, NSEP took on full management of this resource and rebranded it as NSEPnet (NSEP, undated-a).

Additionally, a higher-level organizational change took place in 2012. It merged NSEP with the Defense Language Office to form DLNSEO. The change was to enhance collaboration between the two functions and give DLNSEO a leading role in DoD's policy, planning, and programs for foreign language, culture, and regional expertise. Determining precisely what changed for the Boren Awards program as a direct result of DLNSEO's formation is beyond the scope of this project, but changes were intended and expected. Merging NSEP and the Defense Language Office most certainly produced downstream effects (positive, negative, or mixed) on the newly joined operations of each of the formerly separate offices.

The Boren Network, Alumni Involvement, and Outreach Are Growing

In the last two decades, Boren stakeholders both inside and outside NSEP have taken steps to establish and grow the Boren community. By 2006, Boren alumni had formed an independent alumni group (originally called the Boren Forum and now called the NSEP Alumni Association), and they select fellow Boren alumni to honor with awards. In 2016, NSEP launched the Boren mentoring program to connect Boren awardees returning from study abroad with Boren alumni employed in public service. The program is meant to foster networking among graduating students and employed alumni, help students find jobs to fulfill their service requirements, and strengthen the Boren alumni base. In 2017, NSEP established the official Boren Awards Alumni group on the professional networking platform LinkedIn, and in 2020 it began a podcast series called *NSEPnet Connect!* to highlight the careers of Boren alumni and provide advice to federal job seekers. The Boren network has grown since the Boren Awards' inception, and it holds promise for the future.

Research Approach

Having last surveyed Boren alumni in 2014, Defense Human Resources Activity, DLNSEO, and the Office of the Under Secretary of Defense for Personnel and Readiness asked RAND to evaluate the Boren Awards program by surveying the alumni again. The RAND team design a mixed methods approach to examine the program and Boren awardees' careers. The research leveraged stakeholder discussions, a literature review, and a web-based survey to address the following questions:

- What career paths have Boren alumni taken after completing their degree programs?
- What do Boren alumni report as the strongest influences on their career choices, whether they stayed in government service or transitioned to the private sector?
- What factors facilitate or impede the employment of Boren alumni in DoD and other federal agencies?
- What program improvements would enable Boren alumni to use the skills and knowledge acquired through the Boren program more fully in service to DoD and other federal agencies?

Overview of the Report

The rest of this report provides the findings from this effort and offers recommendations to strengthen the Boren program based on alumni feedback. Chapter 2 describes the research methods and analysis approach in detail. Chapter 3 provides an overview of the survey respondents. Chapter 4 focuses on the student portion of awardees' career paths. Chapter 5 describes alumni career paths, including early and most recent jobs; it also discusses the findings on career choices and plans to remain in the federal workforce. Chapter 6 provides excerpts from alumni comments on their experiences with the Boren program, its value to them, and suggestions for improvements. Chapter 7 provides our findings from the research and recommendations to strengthen the Boren Awards program as it moves forward.

CHAPTER 2

Research Methodology

This chapter describes the project's research methods, which include literature and document review, interviews, survey development, fielding, and quantitative and qualitative data analysis.

Literature and Document Review

To provide context for the research, we began by reviewing information about a prior survey of Boren alumni, which had been conducted by CNA (Wolfanger, Russell, and Miller, 2014) and provided to RAND by DLNSEO. We reviewed literature on the federal workforce and factors that influence individuals' career choices, especially as related to government service. We also reviewed documents specifically related to the Boren Awards program, such as those of the NSEA legislation that authorized it; DLNSEO and NSEP annual reports; and other documents provided on the DLNSEO website (DLNSEO, undated-c).

We focused on literature related to U.S. federal government workforce composition and trends, factors that influence people's interests and choices related to government jobs, and possible relationships between demographic characteristics and career choices. We ran searches through Google and Google Scholar using combinations of various key words and phrases, such as "U.S. government," "career(s)," "choice(s)," "decision(s)," "government," "workforce," "federal," "job(s)," "motivation," "interest(s)," "demographic(s)," "college," and "student(s)," among others. We narrowed the search results by scanning abstracts when available or sections of the documents for relevance.

Interviews

For early qualitative insights about Boren stakeholders' experiences, we conducted interviews with nine Boren alumni who received awards from 2000 to 2018 and five employers who were familiar with the Boren program. The questions are available in Appendix A. The individuals were identified from lists provided to RAND by DLNSEO. The team selected employers to cover a variety of agencies and alumni from across a relatively wide span of years.

Survey Development

DLNSEO wished to build on the prior survey rather than duplicate it exactly or start from scratch. They requested that the new survey be designed to allow for comparison between past findings and new ones, but did not require such comparisons to be part of the present project. To develop the new survey, we consulted with DLNSEO regarding the utility of each of the past questions and topics on which new questions would be added. We also worked with NSEP staff to understand the timing and substance of important events in the program's evolution to identify possible points for disaggregation in the analysis to come. (A timeline of such events is provided in Appendix A.) The draft survey was rigorously reviewed and tested before it was put into action.

The survey collected data on respondents' program-related characteristics, such as degree type, date, and language studied, along with postaward employment, the Boren service requirement, career influences, and awardees' reflections on their experiences as Boren alumni. It used a variety of question types, such as multiple choice, multiresponse options, requirement scales, and open response fields. The survey questions are provided in Appendix B. For the web survey, RAND's survey programmers established skip patterns and dependencies to maximize ease of use for survey participants.

Sample

The survey was fielded to 4,022 Boren Scholar and Fellow alumni in good standing as of early 2022 for whom NSEP had valid email addresses. To be considered in good standing, an individual must have done the following: (1) received a Boren award at any time from program inception to date, (2) completed the Boren-funded study abroad, (3) graduated from the degree program for which they received the Boren award, and (4) fulfilled their one-year government service commitment or met the requirement by completing less than a year of government service and repaying a portion of the award. More than 90 percent of alumni in the sample completed the government service requirement, and less than 10 percent completed part of the government service and repaid a portion of the award. Chapter 3 describes the respondents in terms of their Boren program characteristics, which are consistent with the overall Boren alumni population.

Administration and Response Rate

RAND's Survey Research Group programmed and administered the survey using the web-based survey platform Confirmit. Through Confirmit, they emailed survey invitations to Boren alumni, using email addresses provided by DLNSEO, aiming for a 30-percent or higher response rate. Each contact received an invitation with a unique code that allowed the survey team to remove from further email reminder lists invitees who had completed the survey.

The survey was open for more than two months, from March 9 to May 30, 2023. After the initial March 9 invitation, a total of six follow-up and reminder emails were sent only to those who had not yet completed the survey. The reminders were timed to arrive on varying days of the week, avoiding weekends. Each reminder email was followed by a spike in completed surveys. At the end of the fielding period, the number of completed surveys was 1,232, representing 31 percent of the 4,022 invitations delivered.

Data Analysis

The survey data were primarily quantitative. Some items provided an open response field for "Other" to allow respondents to write in a response if their answer was not among the options provided. The last survey question provided an open-response text box in which respondents could comment freely on their Boren experience.

For the quantitative data, the team calculated frequencies, percentages, and measures of central tendency where appropriate. For each item we calculated the overall result for the entire group of 1,232 completed surveys. For some items, we also examined the results for subgroups—for example, a group defined by the time period in which respondents completed their Boren studies. This kind of analysis made it possible to note whether significant differences existed between the subgroups. We explain the basis for any subgroup analysis with the findings. We used t-tests, chi-square testing, and design-based F testing in the analysis.

For time-based groupings, the cut points were selected in consultation with the DLNSEO and NSEP. In some cases, we divided the responses into two or more groups—for example, those with award dates from the program's inception in 1994 through 2012 in one group and those from 2013 to 2020 in another. The division between 2012 and 2013 recognizes that the job and career experiences of those who participated in the earlier stages of the program might have differed from those who did so later, after legislation updates expanded the special hiring authorities for Boren alumni. The year 2012 was also when NSEP and the Defense Language Office were merged.

Weighting Response Data

Inverse probability weights were developed to compensate for selection bias within the sample of respondents drawn from the broader Boren alumni population. A logistic regression model for response probability was created using award year, award type, program language, country, and program type to create survey weights. These weights ensure that results were representative of the Boren population, and they were used throughout the analysis.

Open-Ended Response Coding

An open response field at the end of the survey allowed respondents to give open-ended comments, such as additional thoughts about the Boren program in their own words. A team of three policy analysts read through the open-ended responses. Each response was broken out into content areas and coded into mutually exclusive categories tied to the Boren program process: Boren Application, Boren Award Experience, Boren Service Requirement, Postaward Education/Education Requirement, and Employment/Service Position. During the process, three additional categories were created: Recommendation, Other, and Not Relevant. In addition to category, each comment was coded for valence: Positive, Negative, or Neutral. Based on the comments within each category, general themes were developed.

The following chapters discuss the findings from these analyses.

CHAPTER 3

Characteristics of the Alumni Surveyed

As mentioned in Chapter 2, the survey collected a total of 1,232 completed responses from the 4,022 Boren Scholar and Fellow alumni invited. This chapter describes the respondent sample according to their Boren program type (Scholar or Fellow), graduation year, language studied, and academic majors. We used the information to confirm that the sample represents the population of Boren alumni on these key dimensions.

Most Respondents Were Boren Scholarship Alumni

As shown in Table 3.1, 56 percent ($n = 686$) of the completed surveys were from Boren Scholar alumni, meaning they received their awards as part of undergraduate degree programs. Boren Fellow alumni, awardees who received their awards during graduate programs, represented 44 percent ($n = 546$) of the sample. The total number of Boren Scholarships awarded exceeds the number of Fellowships (DLNSEO, undated-b); the greater percentage of Scholars than Fellows in the sample is consistent with that.

Respondents Represented Every Award Year from Inception Through 2020

Figure 3.1 shows the distribution of responses by award year. Except for 2020, each award year had at least ten respondents. The lower numbers of responses from the earliest years were not surprising considering the passage of time. Conversely, the lower numbers of responses from the most recent years, especially 2020, could reflect alumni not yet having enough time to build a career path to report on. It is possible that coronavirus disease 2019 disruptions to study

TABLE 3.1
Survey Responses by Boren Program

Boren Program	*N* (%)
Scholar (undergraduate)	686 (56)
Fellow (graduate)	546 (44)
Total	1,232 (100)

FIGURE 3.1

Response Frequencies, by Award Year

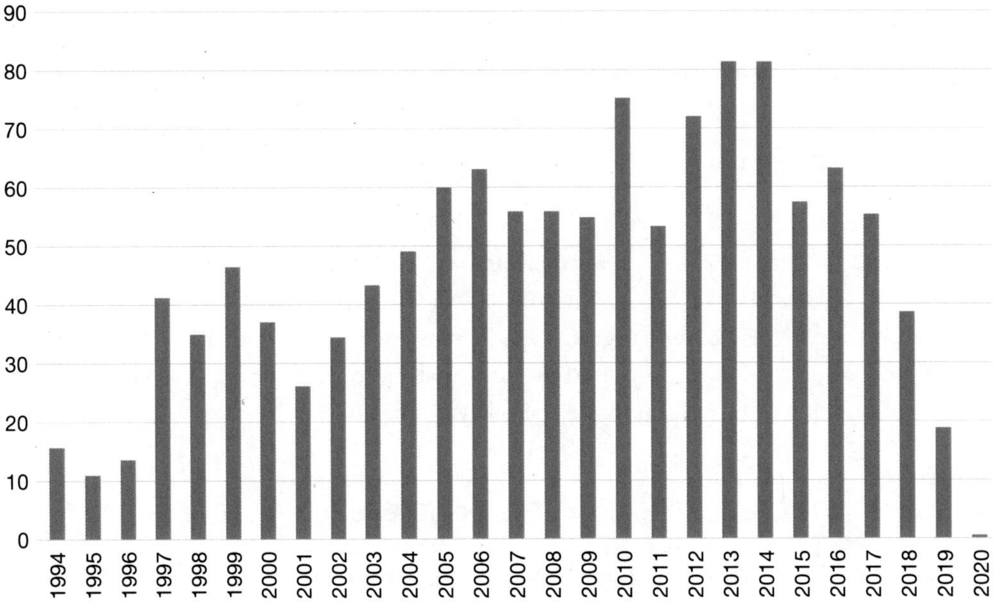

abroad and/or job seeking in 2020, 2021, and part of 2022 could have affected the most recent awardees' readiness for or interest in completing the survey, but we could not tell from the data.

Respondents Had Learned More Than 60 Languages

The survey responses reflected the diversity of languages studied through the Boren Scholarship and Fellowship program. More than 60 languages of study were represented. The top ten languages of study reported overall were Arabic, Mandarin Chinese, Russian, Japanese, Portuguese, Spanish, Swahili, Hindi, Korean, and Turkish (in that order). For the first decade of award years (1994–2004), Russian was the most reported language of study, but it fell to third among respondents from award years 2005 and later. Mandarin Chinese was consistently the second most reported language of study across time periods. Our findings for the top ten languages of study match those reported by DLNSEO almost exactly, differing only in the order of the last three (Hindi, Korean, and Turkish in our survey, versus Korean, Turkish, and Hindi in the DLNSEO reporting).

Respondents Had Studied in More Than 80 Countries

The survey respondents reported overseas study in more than 80 countries overall. The most frequently reported countries overall were China, Russia, Egypt, Jordan, Japan, Brazil,

Morocco, India, Tanzania, and South Korea (in that order). However, looking only at responses for the award years 2013–2020, the most frequently reported countries were China, Jordan, Morocco, Tanzania, Kazakhstan, Brazil, Senegal, South Korea, Japan, Mozambique, and Indonesia (in that order). The representation of Tanzania, Senegal, and Indonesia could be associated with the introduction of Regional Flagship Language Initiatives, starting in 2011, which made study in these three countries, among others, more accessible. Scholarship numbers in Kazakhstan and Morocco also reflect the influx of Boren Flagship Scholars when the Language Flagship program's Russian and Arabic capstone programs were moved out of Russia and Egypt for safety and security issues.

About 8 percent of respondents reported participating in one of the Regional Flagship Language Initiatives established between 2011 and 2019—the African, Indonesian, South Asian, and Turkish Flagship Language Initiatives, respectively. The rest of the respondents (86 percent) reported that they designed their own study-abroad programs. Most respondents (80 percent) reported spending between six and 12 months living and studying in their chosen countries. The most common duration was 12 months, reported by 30 percent. Three percent of the sample ($n = 36$) reported having completed a Language Flagship program while on scholarship through the Boren program.

The Sample Represented a Wide Variety of Majors and Interests

The reported major fields of study and disciplines numbered more than 50 and reflected a diversity of interests. A few were more heavily represented. International affairs was by far the most common, followed by political science, languages and linguistics, area studies, international development, history, economics, business, anthropology, and biology. Public administration, environmental science, and public health were also strongly represented.

When they received the Boren award, most respondents (55 percent) were pursuing bachelor's degrees. About 24 percent were in master's degree programs; 19 percent were in doctoral programs; and 2 percent in J.D., M.B.A., or certificate programs. About 3 percent were in the U.S. military, the reserves, or a Reserve Officers' Training Corps program at the time of their Boren awards. Just more than half (52 percent) reported pursuing additional education later.

Conclusion

The sample of alumni who responded are generally consistent with the descriptions of the overall population of Boren alumni in publicly available information, such as the DLNSEO annual reports and on the Boren Awards website. The strong survey response rate (31 percent) and the general similarities between the respondents and the overall Boren population support viewing the sample as representative. In Chapter 4, we share findings regarding their career interests and influences.

The Boren Career Path from Student to Working Professional

This research investigated numerous stages of a Boren awardees' career path, beginning with exploring educational, funding, and career options and continuing through to their careers as working professionals. In this chapter, we discuss influences during the earliest stages of becoming a Boren awardee—learning about the program and deciding to apply.

Key Stages of Boren Awardee Careers

To facilitate the career-path discussion, Figure 4.1 depicts our notional concept of ten stages along Boren alumni career paths, from student to working professional.

Explore options. Before students decide to apply to Boren, we assume them to be in a stage of learning about their academic and career options, including actively seeking information and receiving information passively from their social and academic networks. This stage is when they learn about the Boren Awards and perhaps other scholarship, internship, and fellowship opportunities.

Apply to Boren. If the Boren program's educational offerings, financial award, federal service commitment, and career opportunity are sufficiently attractive, the student applies. They will interact with the program's administrative and support features at this stage.

Receive award. After application screening, the student receives the news about their award, and they prepare to live and study overseas.

Study overseas. The student travels to their selected country; lives in the local culture; studies language intensively; learns the language and the culture immersively; and acquires international, professional, and life skills from the experience.

FIGURE 4.1

The Boren Awardee's Path from Student to Working Professional

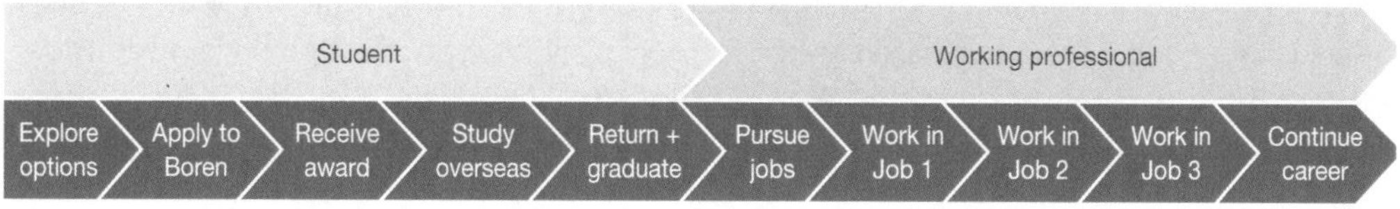

Return and graduate. After completing their study program, the student returns home to the United States, completes their academic program, and graduates. They are expected to begin a job to fulfill the service requirement within three years of graduating if they are scholarship recipients, and within two years of graduating if they are fellowship recipients.

Pursue jobs in the federal government. The recent graduate searches for jobs, networks, and submits job applications. They are expected to seek jobs that meet the Boren service requirement within the congressionally mandated tiers:

- Tier 1 comprises positions in the four priority agencies: DHS, DoD, DoS (including its work with USAID), and the intelligence community)
- Tier 2 includes other federal positions (outside the four priority agencies) with national security responsibilities
- Tier 3 includes positions in U.S.-based education, related to the awardee's NSEP-funded study (language, region, or field of study).

Boren job seekers should use NSEPnet and the federal employment website USAJOBS (USAJOBS, undated). They are encouraged to pursue positions with special hiring authorities, which give them noncompetitive access to career-track (rather than temporary) positions in the federal government. The Boren legislation mandates that Scholars begin qualifying federal service within three years, and Fellows within two years. Once any award recipient has been approved for a service position, they have five years from the date of approval to complete their service requirement in full. They may or may not choose to stay at a single position to complete the requirement.

Work in Job 1. The recent graduate accepts and works in their first job after graduation. For Scholars, it may be their first full-time job. For Fellows, the same could be true, but they might have prior work experience. They work and get paid like any other employee. If the job qualifies, the time in this position counts toward fulfilling the Boren service requirement, and one year of work will fulfill their obligation. If hired with special hiring authorities, they can become federal career-track employees, now with the associated benefits and opportunities. If the job does not qualify, they must still find qualifying federal employment and change jobs within two years of graduating.

Work in Job 2. The working professional secures their second job. If Job 1 fulfilled the requirement, staying in or leaving this second job is entirely up to the individual. Alternatively, if they leave Job 2 before completing their service requirement, they must seek another qualifying job that begins within two years of graduation and work in it long enough to complete a combined total of 12 months across their qualifying federal jobs.

Work in Job 3. The working professional begins their third job. For about two-thirds of Boren awardees, their service requirement has been fulfilled by this time, and they can make job and career decisions solely based on the factors any working professional would consider. For the remaining one-third, depending on their first two jobs' durations, they may be nearing the deadline for the federal service requirement; if this job does not meet the criteria, they are obliged to keep looking for a qualifying job or repay part of the award.

Continue career. By the fourth job, about 80 percent of Boren alumni have already completed their service requirement and are free to make career decisions based on the factors any working professional would consider, such as interests, opportunities, compensation, personal factors, and the like. These working professionals have college or advanced degrees; international experience and/or work experience, including federal government experience; and they have the education, language, cultural, and professional skills to contribute meaningfully as workers and potential leaders. The Boren program would want a high percentage of Boren awardees to continue their careers in federal service with national security responsibilities.

Below we discuss findings related to the first two stages, which determine whether a student, who may have many options, will decide to apply for a Boren Award. Chapter 5 describes jobs and career paths. We did not look in detail at how Boren Awards were allocated, nor at graduation rates, because those topics were beyond the scope of this project.

Students Learned About the Boren Awards Through Various Sources

Nearly three-fourths (74 percent) of the alumni said they were considering seeking federal employment before they learned about the Boren Awards. Learning about the Boren Awards (during the first stage in Figure 4.1) is, of course, the first gateway to possible entry. Knowing students' information sources should help NSEP and other Boren stakeholders design and execute outreach, communications, and networking opportunities to expand the pool of potential applicants. The survey asked alumni how they learned about the Boren program, allowing them to check all that applied on a list of possible information sources. Figure 4.2 shows the findings for the overall responses, and then separated for the early cohort and the recent cohort. The separate findings for the early and recent cohorts are valuable here because the availability and use of some of the sources differed substantially between the earlier and more recent years.

Overall, the most common way alumni learned about the Boren program was through an *academic adviser or faculty member*, endorsed by nearly 60 percent of all respondents, represented by the dark-blue bars. For this item there was no significant difference between the early cohort (light-blue bars) and the recent cohort (tan bars). As faculty members and academic advisers appear to be strong advocates for Boren, DLNSEO might consider increasing outreach to faculty and advisers at institutions where there is already a strong Boren presence and building new inroads to additional academic institutions through targeted promotion of Boren programs to faculty and advisers.

The second most common source was a *DLNSEO or NSEP website*, which was endorsed by 23 percent overall, but significantly more often by the early awardees (25 percent) compared with the recent ones (13 percent). Third overall was through an *other Boren Award recipient*,

FIGURE 4.2
How Respondents Learned About the Boren Awards Program

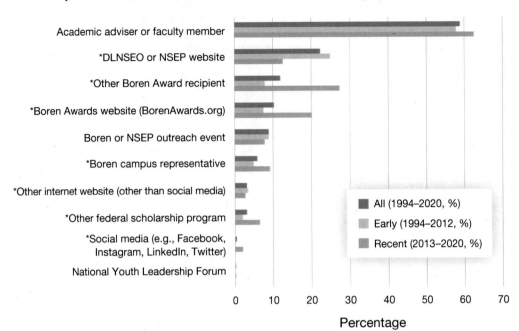

NOTE: *Indicates a statistically significant difference between the early and recent cohorts in the direction depicted (*p* ≤ 0.01).

endorsed by 11 percent overall, but significantly more by the recent cohort (28 percent) compared with the early cohort (8 percent).

In the middle were the *Boren Awards website* (see Boren Awards, undated), *Boren or NSEP outreach event*, and *Boren campus representative*. In the recent cohort, 21 percent endorsed the *Boren Awards website* and 10 percent did so for *Boren campus representative*; those rates were significantly higher than for the early cohort (8 percent for the website and 5 percent for a campus representative), which makes sense because those sources were introduced later and therefore not available to many in the early cohort. The least endorsed sources were *other internet website (other than social media)*, *other federal scholarship program*, *social media*, and the *National Youth Leadership Forum*. Two of these—*other federal scholarship program* and *social media*—were endorsed by alumni in the recent cohort at significantly higher rates. This aligns with the fact that social media emerged around 2006 and thereafter, so alumni from the first 12 or so years of the program could not have used it.

Boren Applicants Were Attracted by Several Program Features, Some Related to Career Interests

After alumni learned about the program as students, several factors attracted them to apply, which is the second stage in Figure 4.1. The factors that were more important to them reflect what influenced their career decisions at this early stage. The survey asked alumni to rate the relative importance of a variety of factors in their decisions to apply for Boren awards. In the analysis, we grouped the responses to determine each factor as either more important or less important. Figure 4.3 displays the relative importance of nine factors. The blue bars represent the percentage of alumni rating that item as more important; the red bars represent the percentage rating it as less important.

As is shown in Figure 4.3, most alumni rated the opportunities for *overseas experience, regional study, funding and support, cultural learning, language study,* and *working in the federal government* as more important influences in their decisions to apply.

The factors they more commonly rated as less important were *becoming part of the Boren network,* the *possibility of receiving mentoring,* and *connecting with my heritage/background.* However, to account for the fact that the Boren network and Boren mentoring were not avail-

FIGURE 4.3

The Importance of Various Factors in Deciding to Apply to the Boren Awards Program

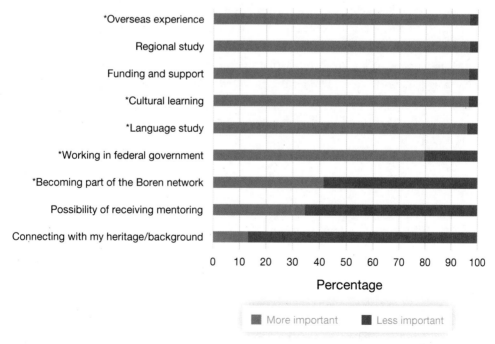

NOTE: *Indicates that the recent cohort (2013–2020) considered this factor significantly more important than did the early cohort (1994–2012; $p < 0.01$).

able to much of the early cohort, we also examined the responses for the early and recent cohorts separately. Doing this revealed that the five factors marked with an asterisk (*) in Figure 4.3 were significantly more important to the recent cohort than the early cohort: *overseas experience, cultural learning, language study, working in the federal government*, and *becoming part of the Boren network*. In fact, 50 percent of the recent cohort rated *becoming part of the Boren network* as more important, compared with 39 percent of the early cohort. This suggests that the Boren network had become more known and more of a draw to potential applicants.

Conclusion

The finding that nearly three-fourths of the alumni surveyed were considering federal employment *before* learning about the Boren Awards suggests that Boren information reached at least some of its intended audience of undergraduate and graduate students already interested in public service. The finding that about one-fourth of the alumni did not consider federal employment before learning about the Boren Awards suggests that the program's features may have attracted students without prior interest to apply and commit to trying federal service for at least one year early in their careers.

The other findings may suggest that personal connection and interaction can be leveraged further to promote the Boren Awards. Academic advisers and faculty members were the most cited source in informing students about the Boren opportunity. It is not surprising that students would take note of information from those in guidance or teaching roles in their institutions. This suggests that higher education staff and faculty are a powerful channel for reaching students, and expanding outreach to people in those roles could draw more students to the Boren opportunity. We also saw that significantly more of the recent cohort, compared with the early cohort, learned about the program from another Boren award recipient. This hints at the growing Boren network's potential and invites strategic efforts to strengthen the Boren Awards network and the brand, which we will discuss in Chapter 6.

CHAPTER 5

Boren Alumni Career Paths

The Boren Awards exist to strengthen the federal workforce by preparing future workers and leaders with international skills, and the career paths of its alumni are important indicators of its effectiveness. If the program is working well, one would expect high percentages of Boren graduates completing their federal service requirements early in their careers and high percentages of Boren alumni continuing in federal jobs for years beyond their service requirements. This chapter synthesizes our findings on Boren alumni career paths and what they suggest about the program's effectiveness. Recalling Figure 4.1, this chapter focuses on the stages after graduating, as shown in Figure 5.1.

Ideally, every Boren awardee would secure qualifying federal employment soon after graduating and work in that job for at least a year to fulfill the service requirement. When pursuing jobs, they have access to various supports, including NSEPnet (NSEP, undated-a), the federal USAJOBS website (USAJOBS, undated), Boren networking events, and self-guided networking with Boren alumni. For some jobs, special hiring authorities allow federal employers to hire Boren awardees noncompetitively, which is meant to make securing qualifying employment easier and faster for both the applicant and the hiring agency.

Boren Scholars have three years from graduation to secure and begin a qualifying federal job; Boren Fellows have two. If their first job (Job 1) does not fulfill the service requirement, they must continue to seek a qualifying position for the next job (Job 2), and so on until their federal service is complete. If they complete only some of the federal service, they must repay a portion of award to the federal government. By design, the service requirement strongly affects Boren awardees' career paths.

FIGURE 5.1
Notional Stages in Being a Working Professional

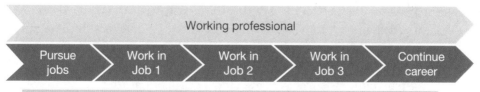

Working professional

Pursue jobs → Work in Job 1 → Work in Job 2 → Work in Job 3 → Continue career

Begin qualifying federal job within two or three years, depending on award type

Most Alumni Surveyed Completed the Service Requirement with Qualifying Employment

About 92 percent of respondents completed the Boren service requirement by working in a job that met the Boren criteria, and 8 percent met the obligation by doing some government service and partially repaying the award. The majority of those who chose partial repayment (55 percent) did so because they pursued employment in a field or position that did not satisfy the service requirement; 34 percent reported not finding qualifying employment by the NSEP service deadline, and 10 percent indicated that other life circumstances or personal commitments were the reason.

Overall, the average time between graduating and fulfilling the service requirement was 3.6 years; it was higher for the early cohort (awardees from 1994 to 2012), at four years, and significantly lower for the recent cohort (awardees from 2013 to 2020), at 2.5 years ($p < 0.001$). Most of the alumni surveyed were Scholars and were required only to *begin* a qualifying job within three years of graduation. These findings are positive and suggest that Boren alumni are, on average, progressing at the expected pace. Further, a significantly lower average time for the recent cohort is positive and may be related to the additional supports provided to Boren job seekers after 2013.

Early Stages of Boren Careers Are Shaped by Securing and Working in Federal Employment, as Intended

The Boren program is designed specifically to influence the early stages of awardees' careers for at least the first few years. Due to practical constraints, a Boren awardee is not expected to satisfy the government service requirement with their very first job after graduation. To work in an agency that has national security responsibilities, they need to obtain a security clearance—a complex process that takes time. While respondents suggested that there were other factors that seemed to be impediments to finding employment in DoD and other federal agencies (e.g., lack of Boren name recognition among federal hiring managers, difficulty aligning interests and education with available positions, etc.), there were several aspects of the program that facilitated their gaining federal employment (such as DLNSEO support, special hiring authorities, and the Boren alumni network).

Because of known impediments, IIE and NSEP staff commonly advise recent Boren graduates to work in other jobs while awaiting their security clearance adjudications, and many do. An article in *Federal News Network* reported the timelines for obtaining top-secret security clearances were both long and increasing: In the fourth quarter of FY 2023, 90 percent of initial top-secret clearance investigations took 115 days on average, and the average for the remaining 10 percent was even higher (Doubleday, 2023). Further, clearance investigations for Boren alumni may take longer due to their extended international travel and contacts.

Despite those factors, a relatively high proportion (41 percent; $n = 505$) did fulfill the service requirement with their first jobs, as shown in Figure 5.2. This finding was both positive and unexpected considering the potential delay for clearances.

A majority (66 percent) of the alumni reported fulfilling the service requirement with either their first or second job, and 13 percent indicated doing so with their third job. For the remaining 21 percent, the awardees either completed it with a fourth or subsequent job or completed part of it and repaid a portion of the award. Finding that nearly 80 percent of awardees fulfilled the service requirement within their first three jobs is positive, indicating that the program brought these globally educated individuals into qualifying federal service *early* in their careers, as the program is designed to do.

Among the 505 respondents who reported fulfilling the service requirement with their first job, 359 indicated the department or agency that employed them. Table 5.1 summarizes those responses.

Fulfilling the service requirement sooner after graduation, rather than later, benefits both the individual and the government but is constrained by practical realities beyond awardees' control, as described above. The individual benefits by gaining federal work experience, which they had expressed interest in when applying for and accepting the Boren award, *and* by fulfilling their obligation to the program early, leaving them free to make career decisions as they wish. The government benefits by bringing internationally skilled, early-career talent into its workforce, as intended, with the possibility of retaining them in federal service if both parties find it satisfactory. The government benefits further by not having to use resources to continue tracking the awardee for compliance. Thus, both the awardee and the government have incentives to facilitate early federal service completion. In this sample, about one-fifth of the alumni met their service requirements with their fourth job or a later one.

Measures to help this smaller subset of awardees complete the requirement sooner would not only make the program more efficient but would also improve those awardees' experiences. The latter point may become increasingly important for the generation of workers entering the workforce through the next decade. As was mentioned in Chapter 1, Gen Z individuals report high levels of stress and anxiety, and they tend to value resources that support mental health and provide flexibility (Deloitte, 2023). If such trends continue, program

FIGURE 5.2

Which Job Satisfied the Boren Service Requirement

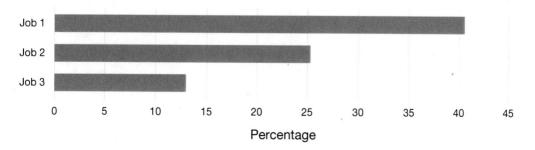

TABLE 5.1

Federal Employers Listed for Respondents Who Secured Federal Positions for Their First Jobs After Graduating

	Agency or Department	Number of Boren Alumni	Percentage
Tier 1	DOS	90	24.9
	DoD	89	24.7
	DHS	51	14.2
	Intelligence community (unspecified)[a]	15	4.3
	USAID	7	2.1
	CIA[a]	6	1.8
Tier 2	U.S. Department of Justice	19	5.3
	U.S. Department of Commerce	13	3.7
	U.S. Congress	9	2.5
	U.S. Department of Agriculture	6	1.8
	U.S. Department of Health and Human Services	6	1.7
	U.S. Environmental Protection Agency (EPA)	4	1.1
	U.S. Federal Judiciary	4	1.1
	Peace Corps	4	1.3
	U.S. Department of the Treasury	3	0.9
	U.S. Department of Veterans Affairs	3	0.8
	National Aeronautics and Space Administration	3	0.7
	U.S. Department of the Interior	2	0.4
	U.S. Department of Transportation	1	0.2
	Federal Reserve	1	0.2
	National Science Foundation	1	0.2
	Other	22	6.1
	Total	359	100

NOTE: Percentages might not sum precisely due to rounding.

[a] The percentages shown for the CIA and other jobs in the intelligence community are likely to be smaller than the actual numbers because some individuals who work in intelligence do not report their status for security reasons.

supports initially designed for such needs in the near term could benefit future Boren award-ees as well.

Among Early Jobs, Alumni Tended to Stay in Service Requirement Positions Longer

We used the career path data to estimate the average duration of each of the first three jobs. The survey did not collect the duration of each job directly, so the analysis roughly estimated this variable based on the length of time between starting one job and starting the next, understanding that the estimate could be flawed if a respondent was not employed for the entire time between starting one job and starting the next. Figure 5.3 shows that the time spent in each job increased progressively from the first to the third job.

We also examined this question conditionally, based on whether the respondent reported using a particular job to satisfy the service requirement. We found estimated tenure in a job to be longer for jobs used to fulfill the service requirement and shorter for jobs not used to fulfill the service requirement. One could reasonably speculate that needing to fulfill the service commitment prompted some awardees to change positions sooner because of the time limit to begin qualifying jobs (three years for Scholars and two for Fellows).

This finding is particularly important and positive because it suggests that service-requirement jobs satisfied their needs in ways that motivated them to stay. It is another

FIGURE 5.3

Alumni Stayed in Service-Requirement Jobs Longer Than Required and Longer Than in Non-Service-Requirement Jobs

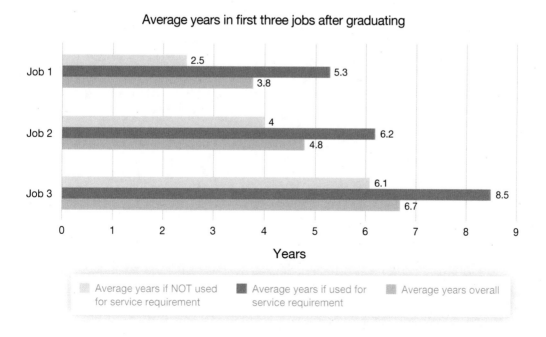

Average years in first three jobs after graduating

Job 1: 2.5 / 5.3 / 3.8
Job 2: 4 / 6.2 / 4.8
Job 3: 6.1 / 8.5 / 6.7

Years

Average years if NOT used for service requirement   Average years if used for service requirement   Average years overall

indication that the Boren Awards are helping to fulfill the purposes in the Boren Act (listed in Chapter 1).

Below we provide insights about the kinds of agencies and jobs the alumni worked in. Table 5.2 displays the numbers and percentages of respondents who indicated which department or agency employed them for their first qualifying federal service job (regardless of when in their career path they started the job).

TABLE 5.2

Federal Employers Listed for Respondents' First Qualifying Federal Service Jobs

	Agency or Department	Number of Boren Alumni	Percentage
Tier 1	DOS	154	25.1
	DoD	141	22.9
	DHS	101	16.4
	Intelligence community (unspecified)[a]	27	4.4
	USAID	23	3.8
	CIA[a]	11	1.9
Tier 2	U.S. Department of Justice	25	4.1
	U.S. Department of Commerce	20	3.2
	U.S. Congress	15	2.5
	U.S. Department of Health and Human Services	11	1.8
	U.S. Department of Veterans Affairs	9	1.4
	U.S. Department of Agriculture	8	1.3
	U.S. Environmental Protection Agency (EPA)	7	1.2
	U.S. Department of the Treasury	7	1.2
	National Aeronautics and Space Administration	5	0.8
	Peace Corps	4	0.7
	U.S. Federal Judiciary	4	0.7
	Millennium Challenge Corporation	2	0.3
	U.S. Department of Transportation	2	0.3
	U.S. Department of the Interior	1	0.1
	U.S. Federal Reserve	1	0.1
	National Science Foundation	1	0.1
	Other	33	5.4
	Total	612	100

NOTE: Percentages might not sum precisely due to rounding.

[a] The percentages shown for the CIA and other jobs in the intelligence community are likely to be smaller than the actual numbers because some individuals who work in intelligence do not report their status for security reasons.

Career Paths After Graduation Suggest Movement Toward Federal Jobs

Looking at the kinds of employment Boren awardees undertook after graduation provides insight into the Boren program's effectiveness in bringing them to, and retaining their skills in, the federal workforce.

As shown in Figure 5.4, almost one-third of respondents (31 percent) reported that their first job (Job 1, represented with the darkest blue bars) was in the federal government. For Job 2 (the medium-blue bars in the figure), respondents were more likely to be in a federal government job (36 percent) than in any other single job type. The same was true for the current or most recent job, which 46 percent of the overall alumni sample reported as being in the federal government. The upward trend in which the likelihood of being federally employed increases with subsequent jobs is positive because the Boren program's goal is to attract awardees to the federal workforce for their careers, not only the one year to which they committed.

FIGURE 5.4

Career Paths After Graduation Show a Trend Toward Federal Government Jobs

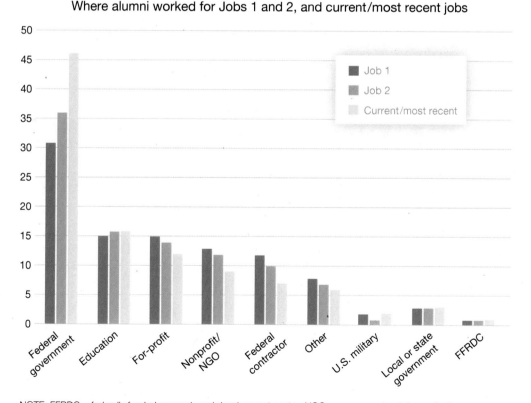

Where alumni worked for Jobs 1 and 2, and current/most recent jobs

NOTE: FFRDC = federally funded research and development center; NGO = nongovernmental organization.

Regarding their *current or most recent job*, just below one-fifth (19 percent) of the early cohort and one-fourth of the recent cohort reported that they were currently employed in the same agency that employed them for their first job after the Boren program. Educational institutions, for-profit and nonprofit organizations, and federal contractors accounted for roughly half of respondents.

Table 5.3 displays the federal employers for the respondents whose last or most recent jobs reported were in federal government *and* who indicated which departments or agencies

TABLE 5.3

Federal Employers Listed for Respondents' Last Reported Federal Jobs

	Agency or Department	Number of Boren Alumni	Percentage
Tier 1	DOS	168	32.0
	DoD	92	17.5
	DHS	74	14.1
	Intelligence community (unspecified)[a]	14	2.7
	USAID	29	5.6
	CIA[a]	7	1.3
Tier 2	U.S. Department of Justice	24	4.6
	U.S. Congress	14	2.7
	U.S. Department of Commerce	12	2.4
	U.S. Department of Health and Human Services	8	1.6
	U.S. Department of Veterans Affairs	7	1.4
	U.S. Department of the Treasury	7	1.3
	U.S. Federal Reserve	5	1.0
	U.S. Department of Agriculture	5	0.9
	National Aeronautics and Space Administration	4	0.7
	U.S. Environmental Protection Agency	4	0.7
	U.S. Department of the Interior	2	0.4
	U.S. Federal Judiciary	1	0.1
	Peace Corps	1	0.1
	Other	48	9.1
	Total	526	100

NOTE: Percentages might not sum precisely due to rounding.

[a] The percentages shown for the CIA and other jobs in the intelligence community are likely to be smaller than the actual numbers because some individuals who work in intelligence do not report their status for security reasons.

employed them in those positions. For the priority, or Tier 1, federal employers, which represented 67.5 percent of the named employers for respondents' last federal jobs, the DOS was the most frequently reported, at 32 percent; this was followed by DoD, at 17.5 percent; DHS, at 14.1 percent; and the CIA and unspecified intelligence employers, at 4 percent (combined). The Tier 2 federal employers accounted for 32.5 percent of those for whom respondents reported the names of departments or agencies.

Job Titles Suggest Career Growth from Early to Current or Most Recent Positions

In addition to job sector, the survey asked for job titles for the first and other jobs held to give insight to the roles the alumni performed at work. The box below shows the job titles reported by at least 3 percent of respondents who reported working in a particular sector. There was a wide variety, but for federal government, federal contractor, and for-profit organizations, the most reported job title was *analyst*. The *analyst* job title appeared in the nonprofit/NGO category too, but *program assistant* was the most common in that sector.

Common Job Titles for First Jobs Suggest Entry- or Midlevel Duties

- Federal government:
  - Analyst
  - Foreign service officer
  - Asylum officer
  - Foreign affairs officer
  - Intern
  - Refugee officer
  - Intelligence specialist
  - Program specialist
  - Intelligence officer
  - Research assistant
  - International trade specialist
  - Passport specialist
  - Fellow
  - Program manager

- For-profit organization:
  - Analyst
  - Customer service representative
  - Engineer
  - Project manager
  - Associate
  - Intern

- Nonprofit/NGO:
  - Program assistant
  - Program associate
  - Research assistant
  - Intern
  - Analyst
  - Fellow
  - Research associate
  - Program coordinator

- Federal contractor:
  - Analyst
  - Associate
  - Consultant
  - Researcher
  - Program assistant
  - Research specialist

As one might expect, those who reported first jobs in an educational institution listed job titles such as *professor* or *teacher* (53 percent), *research staff* (12 percent), or *administrator* (12 percent). The job titles provided by alumni who served in the military, or worked in state or local government or for an FFRDC, were widely varied and too few to report or analyze.

The job titles for respondents' current or most recent job portray a trend toward higher levels of responsibility, management, and leadership roles. The box below displays those job titles. In federal government and federal contractor organizations, *analyst* was again the most reported job title. However, job titles associated with management, leadership, and more responsibility also emerged here—for example, *branch chief, director, diplomat, manager, CEO,* and *vice president.* These job titles reflect career growth compared with those reported for a first job.

Job Titles for the Current or Most Recent Position Signify Roles with Substantial Responsibility

- Federal government:
  - Analyst
  - Foreign service officer
  - Foreign affairs officer
  - Special agent
  - Adviser
  - Immigration officer
  - Attorney
  - Foreign affairs specialist
  - Refugee officer
  - Program manager
  - Asylum officer
  - Investigator
  - Diplomat
  - Program officer
  - Director
  - Branch chief
  - Emergency management specialist
  - Intelligence research specialist
  - Fellow
  - Coordinator
  - Trade specialist

- For-profit organization:
  - Manager
  - Engineer
  - Director
  - CEO
  - Consultant
  - Analyst
  - Vice president
  - Attorney
  - Partner
  - Program manager
  - Head

- Nonprofit/NGO:
  - Director
  - Program officer
  - Adviser
  - CEO
  - Manager

- Federal contractor:
  - Analyst
  - Consultant

FIGURE 5.5

Current or Most Recent Jobs in Federal Service Were Largely at Supervisory General Schedule Levels and in Senior Executive Service

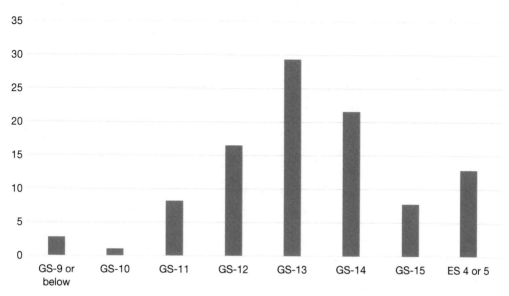

In the same vein, the General Schedule (GS) levels reported for Boren awardees' current or most recent job reflect supervisory positions with greater responsibility, as shown in Figure 5.5. Nearly 60 percent of the 504 alumni who provided GS levels for their current or most recent jobs reported GS-13 through GS-15. Thirteen percent reported jobs in the Executive Service (ES) levels. Combined, nearly three-fourths (72 percent) of these Boren alumni reported holding high-level supervisory or executive leadership positions.

Career Path Influences

The survey asked alumni about the factors that influenced their decisions to accept their current or most recent jobs and how various aspects of the Boren program affected their career paths. Regarding the factors affecting their current or most recent job decisions, Figure 5.6 displays the percentages of alumni who endorsed each listed factor as important in their decision to accept particular positions.

The top factors were *match for your skills* and *expected job satisfaction*, both endorsed as important by more than 80 percent. Just below those two were six factors that were endorsed at rates from 70 to 79 percent: *alignment with your topical interests, location, learning opportunity, alignment with your personal values, benefits,* and *salary*. Three more factors were rated as important by more than half of the alumni: *work/life balance; desire to work in a particular agency, institution, or company;* and *opportunity to expand your contacts and professional*

FIGURE 5.6

Relative Influence of Various Factors on Most Recent Job Decisions

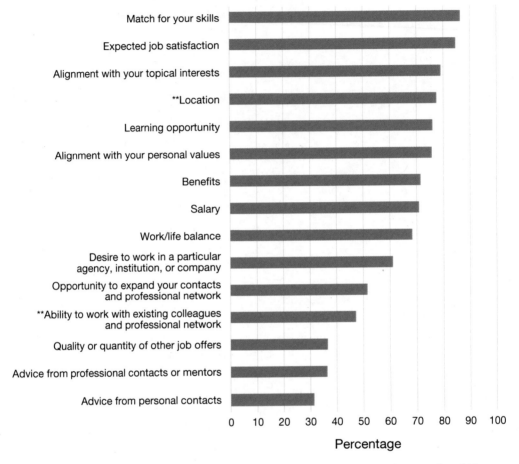

Percentage rating each factor as important in
deciding to accept current or most recent positions

NOTE: **Indicates that the early cohort (1994–2012) considered this factor significantly more important than did the recent cohort (2013–2020; $p < 0.05$).

network. Four items were endorsed as important by less than half of the respondents: *ability to work with existing colleagues and network, quality or quantity of other job offers, advice from professional contacts or mentors,* and *advice from personal contacts.* Two factors were significantly more important to the early cohort compared with the recent one: *location* and *ability to work with existing colleagues and professional network.*

These findings suggest that factors concerning alignment between the job and the person tended to be important (i.e., matching for skills, job satisfaction, topical interests, and values). Also important were considerations about specific advantages the job would provide to the person (i.e., learning, salary, benefits, and location). The finding that *ability to work with existing colleagues and professional network* was more important to the early cohort could be related to Gen Z workers being more inclined to change jobs and careers (Bhaimiya, 2023). That *location* was less important to the recent cohort could also be related to the recent increase in remote and hybrid work opportunities, among many other things.

The survey also asked about how Boren-related skills influenced their career paths. Figure 5.7 displays the findings.

A majority endorsed each listed skill as important to their career paths. This finding suggests that most respondents consider the Boren program to have helped them develop skills that contributed to their career development.

Alumni were also asked about the influence of several Boren features or resources on their career paths. As shown in Figure 5.8, each of the items was endorsed as being influential by less than half of the respondents. However, there were significant differences between the early and recent cohorts on all the features or resources except *eligibility for the DOS's Diplomacy Fellows Program*. The items that received higher rates of endorsements by the recent cohort were *prestige of the Boren Awards*; *Boren Awards name recognition*; *hiring authorities*; *networking opportunities*; *access to the Boren Forum*; and *mentoring from Boren alumni*.

The findings suggest that these Boren program features and resources have increased in value for awardees in more recent years. This further suggests that the increased outreach, network-building efforts, and supports to awardees over the same period may be having positive effects, which have implications for the program's future efforts.

Finally, the survey asked about respondents' intentions to remain in federal service. Figure 5.9 shows that 63 percent of those who responded to this question indicated the

FIGURE 5.7

Relative Influence of Various Skills on One's Career Path

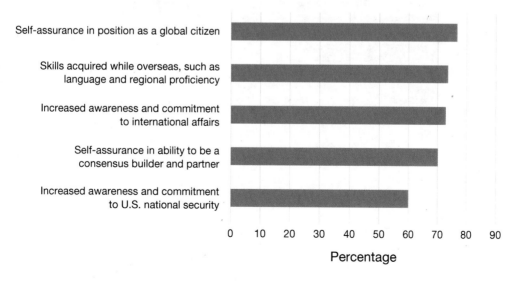

Percentage rating each skill gained through the
Boren Award as influential on their career paths

FIGURE 5.8

Some Boren Program Features and Resources Were Thought to Influence Alumni Career Paths

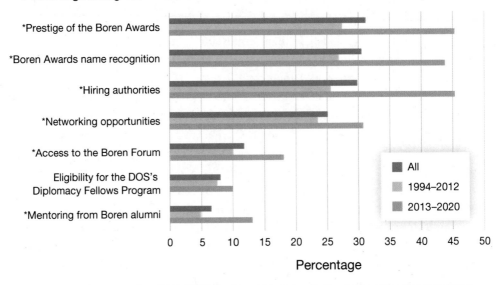

Percentage rating each feature or resource as influential on their career paths

NOTE: *Indicates that the recent cohort (2013–2020) considered this factor significantly more important than did the early cohort (1994–2012; $p < 0.001$ for all, except networking opportunities ($p < 0.05$) and the Boren Forum (now called the NSEP Alumni Association; $p < 0.005$).

FIGURE 5.9

The Majority of Boren Alumni Intend to Stay in Federal Government

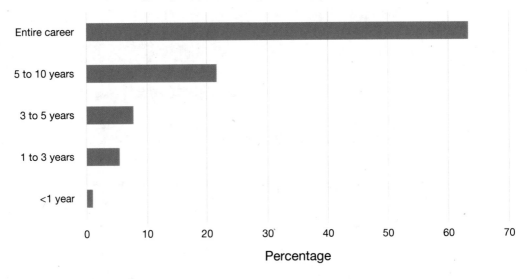

How long do you intend to stay with the federal government?

intention to spend their entire career in federal service, with another 22 percent reporting an intention to stay for five to ten years. This finding is positive: it indicates that a large majority of Boren program alumni intend to devote substantial portions of their careers to federal service, which is what the Boren Awards are designed to achieve.

Conclusion

This chapter describes the career paths of Boren alumni in terms of the time and job changes that transpired before completing their service requirements. It provides estimates of the average time spent in the jobs early in their careers and how that duration differed depending on whether the jobs fulfilled their federal service requirements. It also reveals the sectors in which Boren alumni worked after graduating and the kinds of jobs they worked in. The findings point to strengths and opportunities for improvement.

The finding that 66 percent of the total respondents fulfilled their service requirements with either their first or second jobs is positive, considering that NSEP's legislative mandate provides undergraduates three years from the time of graduation to begin to complete the requirement and graduate students have two years to begin to complete the requirement. Seeing that more recent alumni (2013–2020) completed their service requirements more quickly on average than the early alumni (1994–2012) is also positive, as it suggests that improvements made in assisting graduates have been successful. Although we cannot determine the causes with certainty, the lower average time to completion was associated with a period in which NSEP made changes and added supports to facilitate securing qualifying federal jobs.

The longer duration of employment in jobs that fulfilled the service requirement (compared with those that did not) could be positive if it happens because the awardees consider the qualifying federal jobs sufficiently satisfying to retain them substantially longer than the one year required.

Two findings were notably positive: (1) that most Boren alumni rated their Boren-related skills as important influences on their career paths, and (2) that recent alumni were much more likely than early alumni to rate the Boren program features and resources as influential to their career paths. The latter may reflect the effects of more-recent efforts to improve those features.

While this chapter draws more heavily on quantitative data, Chapter 6 will delve into the qualitative aspects of the Boren program as described by Boren alumni in their comments.

Boren Alumni Perspectives

The final survey item provided an open text box for respondents' comments. This chapter shares a sampling of those comments to add texture and detail to the previous findings and to further illuminate what alumni view as strengths and needs in the Boren Awards program. The positive comments tended to speak to general perceptions of quality and value, while the negative and neutral comments pointed to specific aspects that alumni would like to see improved.

The following section explains how the comments were coded and analyzed. The rest of the chapter shares illustrative comments about the Boren experience, the program offering, and the service requirement; the supports provided to awardees; and the wish for more widespread Boren name recognition. *Each comment should be interpreted as one awardee's perspective or experience and should not be assumed to represent all or even most Boren alumni. They do not represent the views of the RAND authors.*

Comment Coding Overview

In an open response field at the end of the survey, 730 respondents provided comments. These comments, when broken into individual themes, resulted in 1,181 responses for coding. Each comment was coded into only one category:

- Boren Application: comments specifically about experiences applying for the Boren program or the application process generally
- Boren Award Experience: comments about the time spent in the program, including time spent in-country and participating in program activities
- Boren Service Requirement: comments about the requirement specifically, not including comments about a specific placement that satisfied the service requirement
- Postaward Education/Education Requirement: comments referencing the completion of their degree programs after the Boren program
- Employment/Service Position: comments about employment after the Boren program, to include employment aimed to satisfy the service position requirement.

Comments that did not fit into those categories were coded as:

- Recommendation: recommendations made directly about the Boren program
- Other: comments referring to the Boren program that do not fit into the categories listed above
- Not relevant: comments not related to the Boren program.

The most frequently used codes were Boren Award Experience and Employment/Service Position. The coders observed that *positive comments were more general* and tended to reference the award experience. On the other hand, *negative comments tended to be about a specific aspect* of the program. Table 6.1 provides the weighted percentage of comments by category and valence by cohort. The large volume of comment data precludes including them all in this report. Of the 1,181 comments received, 538 were positive (376 from the early cohort and 162 from the recent cohort); 399 comments were coded negative (261 from the early

TABLE 6.1
Comments by Category and Valence, Analyzed by Cohort

Category and Valence	Comments from Awardees 1994–2012 N (%)	Comments from Awardees 2013–2020 N (%)
Boren application		
Positive	0 (—)	0 (—)
Negative	0 (—)	1 (100)
Boren Award experience		
Positive	273 (91)	117 (82)
Negative	22 (8)	25 (17)
Boren service requirement		
Positive	1 (4)	0 (—)
Negative	22 (89)	8 (90)
Postaward education/education requirement		
Positive	3 (100)	1 (100)
Negative	0 (—)	0 (—)
Employment/service position		
Positive	99 (29)	44 (29)
Negative	217 (64)	104 (67)
Recommendations		
Other/not relevant	15 (—)	7 (—)

NOTE: Neutral items are excluded; as a result, columns may not add up to 100%. Data are weighted.

cohort and 138 from the recent cohort); 22 comments were coded Other/Not Relevant, and an additional 222 comments (not included in the chart below) were relevant to Boren but were neutral.

As is shown in the table, the highest volume of comments in any category related to the Boren Award experience overall. These comments were much more likely to be positive than negative for both the early and recent cohorts. Most negative comments tended to be related to employment, including finding jobs to fulfill the service requirement. The findings in Chapter 5 indicated that most Boren alumni fulfill their service requirements in the amount of time expected. Even though the negative comments on postaward employment do not represent all awardees' experiences, they may suggest opportunities to improve this aspect of the Boren experience.

Comments on the Overall Boren Experience Were Positive, and Some Were Effusive

Many alumni commented positively and even effusively about their Boren experience overall, revealing how it has profoundly affected many awardees' lives and careers.

The cohort notation adds context that may help DLNSEO and NSEP understand the effects of changes and program improvements implemented after 2012. Cohort 1 denotes Scholars and Fellows from the early cohort, award years 1994–2012. Cohort 2 refers to those from the recent cohort, award years 2013–2020.

Many alumni commented positively and even effusively about their Boren experience overall, revealing how it has profoundly affected their lives and careers:

> The Boren Scholarship absolutely changed my life. I would encourage anyone who has an interest in studying abroad/learning a language and an interest in serving in the government to consider applying for the Boren Scholarship/Fellowship. Not only was I able to study abroad in [country name], but I was also able to work for the government and provide meaningful service while integrating my linguistic, cultural, and regional understanding of [region name] in a way that furthers U.S. national security interests. (Cohort 2)

> The Boren Scholarship provides important funding to US students to train the next generation of people who can help US national security. Our country's government needs area expertise more than ever. (Cohort 2)

> My Boren Scholarship is solely responsible for every good thing that has happened to me since—both professionally and personally. I met my [spouse], I traveled the world, I collected incredible experiences, and it lit the fuse for my entire career. (Cohort 1)

> Thank you—I feel the Boren program is very important and serves as an important pathway for doctoral or other graduate students . . . [who] consider and choose employment and service with the federal government and in national security positions. This is a very important contribution. (Cohort 1)

These comments and others like them indicate that the Boren program benefited many awardees in ways that are strongly aligned with its intention and purposes.

Many Credited the Program for Advancing Their Careers and Professional Development

Several alumni credited the Boren Awards program with their success: For me the program worked exactly as intended. I did not plan to work for the U.S. government, but I was looking for money to support a study abroad program and NSEP was a great option since I was open to working for the government. When I graduated, I applied for US government jobs ONLY because I had a service requirement. I moved to [Washington] DC and ended up at [agency] specifically to meet the service requirement. Now I'm still there [number] years later, having built a very successful career using critical language skills in various positions directly supporting U.S. national security. For the [money] NSEP paid to help me study abroad for a semester, that's a very decent ROI [return on investment]. (Cohort 1)

The Boren Scholarship was THE driver of my [number]-year career in federal government. I pursued the scholarship due to interest in studying abroad and the service requirement exposed me to careers in the federal government that I would not have necessarily pursued without that requirement. I have had a successful . . . federal career in national security fields that I [100 percent] attribute to the Boren scholarship/service requirement. I plan to remain in the federal government until retirement. I am grateful for this program exposing me . . . as a college student interested in languages and culture . . . to the impactful work one can have representing the United States and working in national security. (Cohort 1)

Though much of the impact is intangible, I believe the Boren has helped me advance in my career and continues to carry prestige. It has played a vital role in developing my skills, offering me new perspective and confidence that helps me in my current position. (Cohort 2)

These comments show some awardees' strong belief that the program played a prominent role in their career success.

Some Described Profound Effects on Their Personal Development

Some alumni described life-changing and transformative effects:

The Boren Scholarship was one of the most impactful and enjoyable opportunities I have had to this point in my life. The program is not perfect, but it is life-changing and I would not trade the experience. I learned a tremendous amount and was exposed to things I otherwise would not have had access to. It is a fantastic program. (Cohort 2)

I grew up quite poor and without the opportunities afforded to me by [this] amazing fellowship program. I would honestly not have the wonderfully fulfilling life I have now. (Cohort 1)

It was a transformative experience that shaped my worldview, helping me to be a better world citizen and giving me life skills/soft skills critical in today's landscape. (Cohort 1)

These comments remind us that workforce development programs not only affect labor statistics and organizational capabilities but can also shape people's lives.

Critiques and Suggestions Related to Specific Elements

Some alumni had suggestions related to the following elements:

- funding amounts
  - "[This amount] doesn't go very far for a semester overseas." (Cohort 2)
- finding a service-requirement position
  - "It was impossible for me to find a role that matched my skills to fulfill my service requirement." (Cohort 1)
  - "The program must do more to ensure Boren award recipients are matched with relevant job opportunities and hired." (Cohort 2)
- stress and anxiety
  - "Fulfilling the service requirement was one of the most byzantine, stressful experiences ever." (Cohort 1)
  - "I will say that the service requirement was very anxiety-inducing, especially as entry-level government positions are difficult to find." (Cohort 2)
- more time to fulfill the requirement
  - "It would have been hugely beneficial if I . . . had [more time] from the end of my program." (Cohort 1)
  - "I understand you can't wait forever for people to fulfill the requirement, but maybe extending the time frame would help some folks." (Cohort 1)

Some Suggested More Supports for Boren Awardees

Other alumni suggested additional career support:

It [the Boren Fellowship] would be improved with greater career support for recently returned Fellows. (Cohort 2)

It would have been invaluable to have one-on-one coaching/mentoring from the Boren office for at least a year. (Cohort 2)

Special Hiring Authorities Can Help When Understood

Some Boren alumni expected more from the special hiring authorities, which are meant to make it easier for federal employers to hire them:

> I never saw a job opportunity to utilize Schedule A. Unsure where to even look to take advantage of the hiring authority. (Cohort 1)

> HR [the Human Resources department] was entirely befuddled by my hiring authorities. (Cohort 2)

But some reported successful use of Schedule A to secure employment[1]:

> I credit the Boren Fellowship with getting me the position I'm currently in (and love) because it allowed the agency to hire me using Schedule A. (Cohort 1)

Alumni Wished for Stronger Boren Name Recognition

Some alumni reported difficulty obtaining employment using the hiring authorities, as they found some federal employers to be unfamiliar with the value of the Boren Awards program:

> I wish the program had more name recognition at the same level as some other State Department programs, I'm frequently having to explain to foreign affairs professionals what the program entails. (Cohort 2)

> NSEP must continue its work to raise the name-recognition of the Boren program within those priority agencies. (Cohort 1)

> I think having Boren Ambassadors in their respective agencies and providing them with off the shelf briefs to provide to their supervisor and hiring manager in their respective organizations would be amazing. The biggest advertisement for the Boren Awards is the alumni. (Cohort 2)

Some Noted a Need for Greater Diversity, Equity, and Inclusion

Some alumni commented on the need to increase diversity, equity, and inclusion in the Boren Program. These comments align with social, federal, and private-sector workplace values, such as those described in *2023 Gen Z and Millennial Survey* (Deloitte, 2023), Executive Order *Establishing a Coordinated Government-Wide Initiative to Promote Diversity and*

---

[1] Schedule A is a special hiring authority that allows federal employers to hire qualified individuals through a noncompetitive process.

Inclusion in the Federal Workforce (Executive Order 13583, 2011), and *Diversity Matters Even More* (McKinsey, 2023).

> Please do outreach at minority serving institutions and reach out to underrepresented groups in International Affairs. I would not have been able to pursue this field had it not been for the overseas experience gained under the program. (Cohort 1)

> More can be done to bring awareness to the Boren Award on community college campuses, so transfer students . . . are aware of it prior to transferring to a 4-year university. (Cohort 2)

> Get more women of color in these programs! (Cohort 2)

> International affairs as a career field could be quite elitist. You [must] have access to a certain amount of money and connections to be successful. For me, the Boren program leveled the playing field a bit. However, the field is sorely lacking in diversity. I would like to see more diverse candidates selected for Boren Awards, that would lead to more diversity, diversity of thought, equity, and inclusion in the international affairs career field. Something that is sorely needed. (Cohort 1)

Some Lamented the Loss of a Complementary Federal Career Program

Some comments expressed disappointment with the suspension of the DOS's Diplomacy Fellows program, which was not part of the Boren program (nor under DoD's control) but complementary to it (see Allen-Ebrahimian and Gramer, 2017). The Diplomacy Fellows Program—started in the early 2000s to help strengthen DOS's talent pool—provided Boren recipients (and awardees from other highly selective fellowship programs) a faster path to employment with the Foreign Service. Some survey respondents considered the program to be an important next step after Boren on the path to joining the Foreign Service:

> One thing that I am disappointed about, however, was the fact that the Diplomacy Fellows Program was suspended. I was also interested in going the Foreign Service route, but the suspension of that program was upsetting because the program was one of the reasons I wanted to apply for the Boren. I know that this is out of NSEP's control, but I just wanted to let you know that this probably negatively hurt many other Boren Fellows' career plans. (Cohort 2)

> The Diplomacy Fellows Program was the key reason I applied for a Boren Fellowship. The fact that the program was cancelled (and still does not exist!) by the time I graduated is still a source of no small degree of resentment. (Cohort 2)

> The Diplomacy Fellows program was the key to getting me into the Foreign Service, and I hope others can similarly benefit from it. Please do all you can to reinstate this excellent opportunity to bring language skills and talent into the Foreign Service. (Cohort 2)

> It's important that the Diplomacy Fellows program be resumed. (Cohort 2)

These comments show that some valued the Diplomacy Fellows Program as an option to complete their Boren service and considered its suspension a consequential loss.

Conclusion

These respondents' open-ended comments paint a picture of a program that has had powerfully positive effects on many awardees and still has room for growth and enhancement. In Chapter 7, we provide recommendations based on these and earlier findings.

Key Findings and Recommendations

This research was designed to shed light on the career paths of Boren Scholarship and Fellowship alumni. DLNSEO and NSEP wanted to better understand awardees' career progress after they completed their service requirements. By surveying Boren alumni from the first awardees in 1994 through 2020, this effort collected valuable retrospective data to understand how Boren awardees have used their skills in the workforce so far. In this chapter, we highlight a few key findings and then offer recommendations to strengthen the program for its wide array of stakeholders.

Key Findings

Boren Alumni Career Paths Align with the Program's Purpose

- Many alumni had positive results from the program, and some describe it effusively as a key factor in their career success.
- Overall, the average time between graduating and fulfilling the service requirement was 3.6 years; it was higher for the earlier cohort (1994–2012), at four years, and significantly lower for the recent cohort (2012–2020), at 2.5 years. This finding suggests that award recipients can not only begin but also complete their service requirements in full in an increasingly short time frame. The shorter time frames were likely facilitated by program modifications—for example, NSEP added Boren-tailored mentoring, career fairs, and job postings to further facilitate Boren awardees' employment in federal jobs.
- Boren alumni tended to stay longer in jobs that satisfied their service commitments. This finding is important because it suggests that service-requirement jobs were satisfying enough to motivate them to stay. It indicates that the Boren Awards are helping to fulfill the purposes in the Boren Act.

The Boren Awards Attracted Students Interested in Public Service to Work in Federal Government, as Intended

- The alumni who were surveyed reported being drawn to the Boren program for the opportunities it offers: travel overseas, language study, regional studies, funding to study abroad, and an onramp to a career in government service.

- Many alumni described valuable experiences that helped them launch successful careers.
- Boren alumni currently working in federal government reported jobs with substantial responsibility and leadership roles.
- Career paths show that alumni became more likely to work in federal government with each subsequent job, and the majority of those working in federal government expressed the intention to remain for their entire career.

Some Alumni Suggested Building More Effective Connections with Employers

- Even though a large majority of alumni satisfied the service requirement within the time allowed, some Boren awardees reported difficulties in doing so. Despite the expanded range of options to fulfill it, and the many supports provided, some awardees struggled.
- Some alumni suggested that NSEP build stronger ongoing relationships between the Boren program and the federal agencies that would benefit from employing Boren talent if only they knew about it. When federal hiring officials know about the Boren program, but their human resources personnel do not, this lack of familiarity can impede the use of the special hiring authorities that would otherwise facilitate employing Boren awardees into federal jobs.
- There are signs of the Boren network becoming more meaningful among recent students and alumni, possibly aided by the increased mentoring, networking, and alumni involvement of the last decade. Survey responses from more recent awardees suggest that they leveraged the Boren network, but many alumni across award years wished the program were more well known among national security agencies.

Recommendations

With those findings in mind, we offer the following recommendations to help DLNSEO and NSEP strengthen the Boren program in its ongoing work to bring the globally enabled talent it cultivates with rewarding federal opportunities to strengthen national security.

Consider Expanding Job Transition Supports for Awardees

The career path findings highlight the stage of *pursuing a job* after graduation as a critical time when some awardees need increased support. The alumni comments suggest that more supports for this career stage may help job seekers and ease the related stress. As discussed in Chapter 5, some alumni comments were often associated with the difficulties they experienced in finding a job that fulfilled the federal service requirements.

Even though around 90 percent of the Boren alumni sample completed their federal service, many expressed concerns over the stress related to finding the right job within the time allotted. Boren has clearly been a strong pipeline, bringing talented individuals into government service, but younger U.S. workers in general are gravitating away from federal government jobs (Jones, 2020), as noted in Chapter 1. While applications to the Boren Awards might not presently be affected by changing generational attitudes, external workforce trends across the federal government suggest that NSEP should consider the potential effects that changing attitudes could have on the future pipeline. In an international survey, workers considered part of the millennial generation and Gen-Z expressed being stressed and burned out (Deloitte, 2023). Relatedly, they tended to prioritize mental health and work/life balance more strongly than did prior generations of workers (Deloitte, 2023). This suggests that additional support services and personalized communications that inspire Boren job seekers and foster persistence will be more helpful than traditional supports that simply transmit information.

Many supports are already in place, such as a robust six-month mentorship program started in 2016, and the annual Boren Seminar and Career Fair. Additional supports might include small-group career coaching (led by a certified coach familiar with federal government contexts), or regular virtual drop-in office hours and/or coffee chats in which current job seekers connect with certified career coaches, Boren advisers, and/or alumni in an informal, low-stress format. There may also be demand for one-on-one support to job seekers facing obstacles they feel ill equipped to dismantle.

As a starting point, NSEP could inventory and review the existing support resources and services to identify the extent to which supports are utilized and which ones are received as most helpful. Conducting focus groups with awardees who graduated in the most recent one to three years could be useful. Making service completion more attainable, and sooner, for a larger share of Boren job seekers could have far-reaching effects by reducing stress for new workforce entrants and accelerating their movement toward federal jobs that need their skills and in which they are more likely to continue to succeed.

Draw from Business-Strategic Communication Approaches to Further Develop and Disseminate Boren's Value to Key Stakeholders

Many Boren alumni lamented the Boren program's lower name recognition when compared with other programs with higher visibility among employers. Their comments called for "marketing" (in the sense of advertising), "publicizing," and "raising awareness," which are all worthwhile but not enough to make impactful, long-lasting impressions with many federal employers. In fact, IIE already conducts substantial outreach and advertising to potential candidates and those who might influence them, while NSEP leads outreach to organizations and individuals who would value the service of a Boren graduate, such as federal hiring officials. Despite these existing efforts, the Boren program does not have widespread name recognition, as many respondents remarked. This suggests a need for a more comprehensive and strategic approach.

We recommend that IIE and NSEP pursue a business-strategic approach to marketing, which would by definition involve more than just advertising. A comprehensive, strategic approach to marketing would more clearly articulate and refine the activities, entities, and processes needed to create, communicate, and deliver an offering that provides value to its stakeholders and society (American Marketing Association, 2013). Further, this kind of business-strategic approach to marketing would treat branding as much more than selecting a name or a logo; it would involve establishing a distinct brand identity and aligning the program's public image with that brand identity so that stakeholders have a consistent, positive association with it (American Marketing Association, 2013). Initial steps could be to articulate the less tangible features of the Boren program that make it distinct and special, such as mission, values, ethos, and a value proposition that would make Boren alumni stand out among other programs' scholars and fellows in the eyes of targeted employers.

Having reviewed a wide selection of DLNSEO and NSEP materials, the Boren legislation, and numerous analyses of it, the RAND team is familiar with the attributes of the Boren opportunity for both employers and students. The program's value needs no embellishment, but it does need strategic, targeted communications that engage and support each of its stakeholder audiences—which are part of branding. The Boren stakeholder groups include

- federal employers in defense and national security
- college and university faculty
- students
- families of prospective and existing Boren awardees
- Boren alumni.

Each of these groups is an important audience for Boren program communications, and each one needs (at least) an easy-to-find entry point to the Boren program that engages them with the program's value and motivates them to become more involved and continue in the program. Noting that faculty members and academic advisers were the most common source through which respondents learned about the Boren program (see Chapter 4), NSEP could strengthen its communication and engagement with college and university faculty to help them spread the word to their students.

A starting point for strategic, targeted communication could be a redesigned and rebranded Boren Awards website. University, NGO, and company websites commonly recognize their various audiences and communicate with them directly with tailored content, through links labeled "For Students," "For Faculty," "For Employers," "For Alumni," and the like. The existing Boren Awards website (Boren Awards, undated-a) speaks to *students* as the primary audience, with a nod to campus representatives as a secondary audience. A more robust approach would be to develop curated content for each of the program's key stakeholder groups. Ideally, the content would inspire affinity. For example, content that commends professors and academic advisers for developing future leaders could evoke a sense of validation that draws them more personally to the Boren program.

A redesigned, audience-centered, content-rich website could be an effective tool to communicate the Boren program's value and engage stakeholders with it. Further, a thorough and effective redesign process would be built around the business-strategic approaches mentioned, such as providing value to stakeholders, and establishing and aligning the program's identity and public image. Such a process may involve a nontrivial investment of resources. Until those resources become available, carefully planned, incremental improvements to Boren outreach, supports to stakeholders, and the existing website could serve to engage more audiences with the Boren program's value and strengthen its brand.

The website could eventually serve as a portal through which job applicants might equip hiring managers with practical information to inspire them to use the special hiring authorities, post job openings through NSEP, and more.

Build Values of Inclusion, Equity, and Diversity into Boren Practices

The Boren program has already taken action to increase diversity, equity, and inclusion among and for its applicants and awardees. Boren program representatives presently conduct outreach to minority-serving institutions as part of the program's university outreach. NSEP reports that Boren awardees represent more racial diversity than the general study abroad population (DLNSEO, 2023). As was noted in Chapter 1, diversity, equity, and inclusion are more important to the generation of individuals currently entering the workforce, Gen Z, than to any generation before them. Along these lines, some alumni remarked on the limited diversity, equity, and inclusion in the Boren program. They recommended stepping up outreach to minority-serving institutions and community colleges and increasing the percentage of women of color. One comment noted the lack of diversity among Boren awardees and said that diversity is "sorely needed." These sentiments comport with generational trends regarding greater value for diversity, equity, and inclusion.

As is true for many other programs and institutions, the Boren program will need continued actions to improve in these areas. The DLNSEO is guided by federal policies and strategies on diversity, equity, inclusion, and accessibility (DEIA), such as those stated in:

- Executive Order 13583, "Establishing a Coordinated Government-Wide Initiative to Promote Diversity and Inclusion in the Federal Workforce" (Executive Order 13583, 2011)
- Executive Order 14035, "Diversity, Equity, Inclusion, and Accessibility in the Federal Workforce" (White House, 2021a)
- the *2021 Government-Wide Strategic Plan to Advance Diversity, Equity, Inclusion, and Accessibility in the Federal Workforce* (White House, 2021b)
- other documents publicly available through the U.S. Office of Personnel Management (OPM) Office of Diversity, Equity, Inclusion, and Accessibility webpage of reference materials (OPM, undated-a).

As a start, NSEP could clearly define and post its position on diversity, equity, and inclusion on the Boren Awards website and provide statistics and information that might encourage a more diverse pool of candidates to apply. Further, decisions that affect equity and representation in the Boren program should be shaped by inclusive practices, such as those laid out in *Promising Practices for Diversity, Equity, Inclusion, and Accessibility in the Federal Workforce* (OPM, undated-b).

Invigorate and Grow the Boren Community Around a Shared Ethos

The two recommendations above and this third one are complementary and intertwined with one another. Those above feed into invigorating and growing the Boren network. The first would support and empower Boren awardees—the program's first and most essential stakeholders. Without the awardees and their skills, expertise, and commitment, the Boren program would have little to offer. The second recommendation would acknowledge the other critical stakeholder groups and implicitly bring them into the Boren sphere, a system in which they can play vital roles in the program's continued success, the quality of the federal workforce, and the nation's security. These activities should be informed by a clear, succinct statement of the Boren Awards' ethos—a set of values and professional characteristics that Boren community members support, promote, and share. These values and professional characteristics could then be used as the foundation of the Boren brand in program decisions and internal and external communications.

The existence of the Boren ethos was recognized by some alumni; one respondent said, "The Boren Scholarship's ethos and focus was a key driver of my professional development." Others mentioned the value they derived from being part of the "Boren community." We recommend that NSEP define what the characteristics are that make the Boren community and the Boren ethos different from other programs and use those characteristics to generate additional interest and awareness of Boren's contributions to national security.

Boren Awards Program Timeline of Events

This appendix provides a timeline of key events from the establishment of the Boren Awards and continuing through past and recent developments. Based on information provided by NSEP, the first two columns in Table A.1 present the year and a brief description of each event. The third column notes whether an event in the timeline represented an update or change to any of four key aspects of the Boren Awards, as follows. The abbreviation *SR* refers to the Boren *service requirement. AS* refers to *administration and support*: the administration of the Boren Awards program and/or the support services provided to Boren Scholars, Fellows, alumni, and federal employers. *NC* denotes *network and communications*: the Boren Awards' network, outreach, and communications. *PO* denotes *program options* for study, such as program updates that expanded Boren awardees' options for pursuing language and regional studies.

TABLE A.1

Key Events for the Boren Awards Program, 1991–2020

Year	Event	Type of Change(s)[a]
1991	NSEA is established, laying the foundation for the Boren Scholarships and Fellowships.	
1994	The first cohort of 317 Scholars and Fellows begins the program, representing 153 U.S. institutions of higher education.	
	The Scholarship Program is administered by IIE; the Fellowship Program is administered by the Academy for Educational Development.	
	The Fellowship Program is administered by the Academy for Education Development.	
	Legislation requires Boren Fellows whose awards cover 12 or more months of study abroad to complete service requirements by working in federal positions related to national security or in U.S. higher education institutions.	SR
1995	NSEP assesses needs in federal national security agencies for individuals with "global skills" based on their knowledge of world regions, languages and cultures, and field of study.	

Table A.1—Continued

Year	Event	Type of Change(s)[a]
1996	Updated legislation now requires Boren Scholars and Fellows to complete service requirements equal to the length of their award-funded studies abroad. This policy continues until 2004.	SR
	NSEP initiates language proficiency testing for all Boren Scholars and Fellows when they return from study abroad.	
1998	At the first Annual Symposium of Boren Fellows, fellowship awardees present the research they conducted while on Boren-funded study abroad.	NC
	NSEP and the OPM release NSEP-NET online as a job portal for Boren awardees seeking federal employment and a searchable résumé database for federal hiring officials to use during recruitment.	AS, NC
2001	NSEP rebrands NSEP-NET as NSEPnet and launches a new website. NSEP administers the website in-house.	AS, NC
2002	NSEA is amended to include the National Flagship Language Initiative providing that "institutions of higher education shall establish, operate, or improve activities designed to train students in programs in a range of disciplines to achieve advanced levels of proficiency in those foreign languages that the Secretary identifies as being the most critical in the interests of the national security of the United States" (Public Law 102-183, 105 Stat. 1271, as amended).	
2005	Congress amends NSEP's legislation. Boren Scholars and Fellows must now complete service requirements of 12 months or longer, depending on the length of their studies abroad. The service must be in DoD or the intelligence community.	SR
	NSEP continues to hold a convocation prior to Boren Scholars' and Fellows' departure to their countries of study, but replaces its small regional convocations with a larger, mandatory orientation in Washington, DC.	NC
	The Secretary of Defense realigns NSEP to be fully integrated into the Office of the Under Secretary of Defense for Personnel and Readiness, where responsibility for language oversight resides. NSEP becomes administratively attached to the National Defense University.	AS
2006	In the first Boren alumni awards ceremony, the Sol Linowitz Award and the Howard Baker, Jr. Award are given out. The awardees are selected and honored by the new, independent NSEP Alumni Association (formerly called the Boren Forum).	NC
	Administration of the Boren Fellowships is transferred from the Academy for Educational Development to IIE. IIE transfers monitoring of the NSEP service requirement to the NSEP Service Team.	AS
2007	Congress amends NSEP's legislation to add options to the service requirement. As before, all Boren Scholars and Fellows must complete service requirements equal to 12 months or longer, depending on the length of their studies abroad. But they may now complete the service requirement in one of the four priority areas of government or in other federal agency positions with national security responsibilities. A further option is added to waive the service requirement in cases of extreme hardship, medical disability, security clearance denial, or hiring freezes.	SR
	Close to 1,500 NSEP award recipients have fulfilled or are in the process of fulfilling their service requirements.	

Table A.1—Continued

Year	Event	Type of Change(s)[a]
2008	Congress amends NSEP's legislation, which adds further options to the service requirement. As in 2007, all Boren Scholars and Fellows must still complete service requirements equal to 12 months or longer, depending on the length of their studies abroad, but they may now complete the service requirements in (1) one of the four priority areas of government, (2) other federal agency positions with national security responsibilities, or (3) positions in (U.S.) education related to the language, region, or academic area they studied with Boren funding. The third option is available if an awardee showed good faith in applying to positions in the federal government before applying to receive credit in the field of education. Consideration for the option to waive the service requirement in cases of extreme hardship, medical disability, security clearance denial, or hiring freezes now considers the length of the awardee's award-funded study abroad. This policy continues from 2008 onward.	SR
2009	President Barack Obama signs new legislation, the NDAA for FY 2010, which directly affects the hiring of NSEP award recipients. It allows that an awardee who has not fulfilled their service requirement may be appointed to an excepted service position with certain authorized federal organizations. If an award recipient is currently working for the federal government in an excepted service position, NSEP can convert the recipient to a new appointment under the NDAA to take advantage of the noncompetitive conversion to career or career-conditional status after two years. Arabic is the top language of study among Boren recipients, followed by Chinese.	SR
2010	The Intelligence Authorization Act of 2010 adds a provision sponsored by Representative Daniel Boren to establish a pilot initiative to increase the number of American students learning African languages. The program is designed to provide additional domestic and overseas options for Boren Scholars and Fellows to learn any of five African languages.	PO
2011	NSEP initiates the African Flagship Languages Initiative program, through which Boren Awardees are provided support to participate in intensive domestic summer institutes followed by overseas language immersion.	PO
2012	NSEP merges with the Defense Language Office to create the DLNSEO. The change is meant to enhance and support collaboration within DoD. DLNSEO plays a leading role in DoD's strategic direction on policy, planning, and programs for foreign language, culture, and regional expertise.	AS
	The Obama administration introduces the "Pivot to East Asia" strategy. East Asia is the top region of study among Boren recipients, surpassing the Middle East and North Africa.	
	President Obama signs into law an expansion of the NDAA for FY 2010 legislation's hiring authorities. In the NDAA for FY 2013, NSEP award recipients who are serving in a term or temporary appointment—or who have less than a one-year break in service—can be reappointed to the excepted service with noncompetitive conversion eligibility. All NSEP awardees serving in temporary or term appointments—regardless of whether they have completed their service requirements—are eligible to utilize this hiring authority.	SR
2014	The Defense Intelligence Agency, in partnership with NSEP, designs, advertises, and launches an internship program exclusively for recently graduated Boren awardees. The program allows interns to gain work experience in research, report writing, briefing development and delivery, policy writing, and intelligence analysis. Those selected are appointed for a one-year period and eligible for a salary and full government benefits.	AS, NC, SR

Table A.1—Continued

Year	Event	Type of Change(s)[a]
	The Middle East and North Africa is the top regional destination among Boren recipients, surpassing East Asia and Southeast Asia.	
2016	The Boren mentoring program begins. Boren Scholars and Fellows returning from study abroad are matched with midlevel Boren alumni serving in the public sphere. The purpose of the mentorship effort is threefold: to strengthen the Boren alumni base, to support networking within the Boren community, and to help NSEP awardees fulfill their federal service requirements.	AS, NC
	East Asia is the top region of study among Boren recipients, surpassing the Middle East and North Africa, beginning the trend of increased attention to East Asia and Mandarin Chinese.	
	Boren awardees can now learn Hindi and Urdu through NSEP's South Asian Flagship Language Initiative.	PO
2017	DoD Instruction 1025.02 renews DoD policy, assigns responsibilities, and prescribes procedures and requirements for administering and executing the NSEP service requirement in accordance with Sections 1901-1912 of Chapter 37 of Title 50, United States Code (Department of Defense Instruction 1025.02, 2017). It also modifies requirements related to the NSEP service requirement and assigns oversight of NSEP to DLNSEO.	AS
	NSEP expands its social media presence to include the official Boren Awards Alumni group on LinkedIn.	NC
	Boren awardees can now learn Indonesian through the Indonesian Flagship Language Initiative (IFLI).	PO
2019	Boren awardees can now learn Turkish through the Turkish Flagship Language Initiative (TURFLI).	PO
2020	NSEP establishes and publishes the "Boren Around the World" podcast to highlight alumni careers and provide federal job search advice and tips.	NC
	As of 2020, 4,238 Boren awardees fulfilled their service requirements.	

SOURCE: Data provided to RAND by NSEP.

[a] Denotes changes to selected aspects of the program.

Interview Protocols

This appendix reproduces the interview questions used for the semistructured interviews with Boren alumni and with federal government employers familiar with the program.

Boren Alumni Interview Protocol

Thank you for agreeing to speak with us. As we explained, we're conducting a research project for Mr. Thomas Constable, Acting Assistant Secretary of Defense for Readiness, and DLNSEO, the Defense Language and National Security Education Office. They have asked RAND to conduct an evaluation of the Boren Scholarship and Fellowship Awards program to look at how the Boren program affects the careers of recipients and the talent pipeline of those with proficiency in critical languages, regional expertise, and cultural knowledge to jobs in the U.S. federal government.

We would like to talk with you about your experience with the Boren program, the experience of securing federal employment, and the factors that have affected your career decisions since your Boren experience.

Background

1. Could you tell us when you received your Boren Award, the region and language you studied, your educational institution, and when you completed your Boren service?
2. What degree were you pursuing when you entered the Boren program, and in what field of study?
3. Did you participate in one of the Regional Flagship Initiatives, or did you design your own program?
4. What is your current job (title, position, responsibilities)?

Experience with the Boren Program

5. How valuable was your experience with the Boren program to your career?
6. In what ways did participating in the program benefit your career?
7. Was there any way in which participating in the program held you back?
8. What changes would you recommend to make it more effective, or to give Boren recipients a better experience?

Language, Culture, and Regional Expertise Gained During the Program

9. How did the Boren program affect your language proficiency and cultural knowledge?

10. What effect, if any, did the Boren program have on developing and obtaining other skill sets?
    - For example: leadership, flexibility, resilience, dealing with adversity, communication skills, critical thinking, teamwork.

11. How effective was the Boren Awards program in helping you learn more about your assigned region?

12. What aspects of the program enhanced your learning about the region?

13. Were there any aspects of the program that limited learning about the region?

14. Is there anything that you wish you learned about the region that you didn't?

Post–Boren Awards Program Career Path

15. How did the Boren Award program influence your career path?
    - Choice of where to work
    - Choice of what kinds of positions to take
    - Amount of time working in (or in support of) the federal government

16. What kinds of jobs have you held since participating in the Boren Award program? Have you worked in government service, and, for how long?

17. What were your career aspirations before you started the Boren Award program? To what extent has your career matched that?

18. To what extent have you used the skills you gained during the Boren Award program in your career?

Government Employment Since the Boren Award Program

19. If you have completed a year (or more) of government employment, how would you describe your experience of working for the federal government?

20. How easy or difficult was it to transfer between positions within the federal government?

21. What are the main skills you use in your daily work? To what extent were these skills developed through the Boren program?

Transfers Between Government and Contractor Positions

22. We understand that sometimes people choose to work in the government as an avenue to transition to contracting positions, and sometimes vice versa. Have you observed this, in either direction?

23. From what you've observed, what are the barriers and facilitators to moving from contracting to government?

Teaching Positions

24. One of the options in the Boren program is to fulfill the service commitment through teaching. Did you consider this option?

Wrap-Up

25. Is there anything else you'd like to tell us about your Boren experience and its effect on your career that we haven't covered?

Boren Employer Interview Protocol

Thank you for agreeing to speak with us. As we explained, we're conducting a research project for Mr. Thomas Constable, Acting Assistant Secretary of Defense for Readiness, and DLNSEO, the Defense Language and National Security Education Office. They have asked RAND to conduct an evaluation of the Boren Scholarship and Fellowship Awards, within NSEP, the National Security Education Program, to look at how the Boren program affects the talent pipeline of people who have proficiency in critical languages, regional expertise, and cultural knowledge working in the U.S. federal government, as well as how it affects the careers of Boren recipients.

We would like to talk with you about your experience recruiting and working with Boren Award recipients.

Background

1. To start, could you tell us about your role within [name of agency]?
2. How long have you been in [this agency] and in this role?
3. In your role, how do you interact with the Boren program and the Boren recipients who come to your agency? How did you learn about the Boren program?
4. Have you worked for other federal agencies previously? If so, can you comment on the same questions for the other agency or agencies?

General Hiring and Skills

5. When recruiting top talent (not specific to Boren), what skills are you looking for?
   a. Conversely, what critical skills do you find some or many applicants lacking?

Recruiting Boren Recipients

6. How did you first learn about the Boren program?
7. What recruiting mechanisms does your agency use to recruit for the positions that would be good matches for a Boren recipient?
   a. Which of those seem to be the most effective overall, and which are most effective in reaching Boren recipients?
   b. About how many Boren recipients were hired by your agency within the last year?
   c. Is that a good number? Would you like it to be different?
8. Does your agency use special hiring authorities in your hiring processes?
   a. If so, how familiar are you with NSEP's special hiring authorities Schedule A (r) and NDAA'13 [National Defense Authorization Act for Fiscal Year 2013]?

9. What has your experience been like using NSEP-specific recruiting tools, such as the NSEPnet job board and résumé database?
    a. Have you had any interactions with the Boren Service Team in the course of hiring Boren recipients?
10. Are there any barriers to recruiting Boren recipients for full-time jobs at your organization?
    a. Can you provide some examples?
    b. Have Borens needed security clearances, and how easy or difficult has it been to obtain them?

Characteristics of Boren Recipients

11. What have you observed about how Boren recipients compare to other employees in terms of knowledge, skills, competency, and professionalism?
12. What are the advantages to hiring them? And the disadvantages, if any?

KSAOs of Boren Recipients [1]

13. What kinds of skills do Boren Award recipients typically bring to your agency?
14. Based on Boren recipients you've interacted with, how knowledgeable are they about the politics, trends, and local issues of the regions or countries they studied?
    a. Are there issues or areas on which they need more knowledge or skills?
    b. How do they use their knowledge to support the work at your agency?

Career Paths of Boren Recipients

15. Based on what you have observed, how long do they usually stay in government service?
16. When Boren awardees have left your agency for new jobs, what kinds of organizations have they gone to?
17. What have been the main reasons that Boren recipients left jobs in your agency?
18. Are there any specific barriers to retaining Borens at your agency?

Transfers Between Contractor and Government Positions

19. We understand that sometimes people choose to work in the government as an avenue to transition to contracting positions, and sometimes vice versa. Have you observed this, in either direction?
    a. From what you've observed in your own experience or from others, what do you think the barriers and facilitators are for someone to move from contracting to government?

Wrap Up

20. Is there anything else you'd like to tell us about your experience employing Boren recipients that we haven't covered?

---

[1] KSAOs = knowledge, skills, ability, and other characteristics.

Survey Protocol

This appendix provides the questions used in the Boren alumni survey. As explained in Chapter 2, the survey used a variety of question types, such as multiple choice, multiresponse options, requirement scales, and open response fields. For the web survey, RAND's survey programmers established skip patterns and dependencies to maximize ease of use for survey participants. In use, the survey presented each participant with questions based on their prior responses, so each participant was asked only a subset of the questions below, and no participant was presented with every question.

Boren Scholarship and Fellowship Survey

Principal Investigators: Jennifer Li (jennifer@rand.org) and Rich Girven (rgirven@rand.org)

Hello and thank you for your interest in this survey! You are being invited to participate in a study conducted by the RAND Corporation, a nonpartisan, not-for-profit research organization. Your participation is **voluntary**. The study team is available to answer any questions you may have related to participating.

The research study is being conducted to learn more about how the **Boren Awards program** affects recipients' careers to gauge program effectiveness and identify ways to improve the program.

If you agree to participate, you will be asked to **respond to a survey** about your experiences, impressions of the Boren Awards program, and your career path. The survey will take approximately 15 minutes.

We do not anticipate any individual risks or benefits with participating in this survey. We do anticipate benefits to the Boren Awards program, thanks to your participation. At the end, we will provide recommendations to the Defense Language and National Security Education Program that may improve future Boren Award recipients' experiences, particularly if we identify qualities of the program that you and other participants identify as particularly beneficial or in need of improvement.

Eligibility. To participate, you must be an alumna/us of the Boren Awards program.

Privacy and Confidentiality. Any identifiable information that you choose to provide will be kept strictly confidential. Participants' individual answers will not be shared with the Boren program except in aggregate.

Questions/Concerns? If you have any questions or concerns about the survey, please contact the research team at BorenProject@rand.org.

If you have questions about your rights as a research participant or need to report a research-related injury or concern, you can contact RAND's Human Subjects Protection Committee toll-free at (866) 697-5620 or by emailing hspcinfo@rand.org. If possible, when you contact the Committee, please reference Study #2020-N0678.

Do you understand and consent to these terms?
Yes—take me to the survey
No [exit survey]

Agency Disclosure Notice:
OMB CONTROL NUMBER: 0704-0646
OMB EXPIRATION DATE: 02/28/2026

The public reporting burden for this collection of information is estimated to average 30 minutes per response, including the time for reviewing instructions and responding to this survey. Comments should be sent electronically to the docket listed below. Please submit electronically at the Federal Rulemaking Portal: https://www.regulations.gov and reference 32 CFR part 236, Docket ID: DOD-2019-OS-0112 and/or by Regulatory Information Number (RIN) 0790-AK86.

[Begin survey]
D1.   Which of the following did you receive? If you received more than one Boren Award, please answer for the most recent.
  – Boren Scholarship (undergraduate)
  – Boren Fellowship (graduate)
  – I have never received a Boren Scholarship or Fellowship

DS1. In what year did you receive the Boren Award?
DS2. For which language did you receive the Boren Award?
DS3. In which country did you use the Boren Award?
DS4. In which Boren Study Program did you participate?
DS5. For what amount of time were you funded to study abroad?
DS6. What degree were you pursuing at the time of the award?
DS7. In which discipline was the degree?
DS8. In what year did you complete the degree you were pursuing during the Boren Scholarship?
DS9. In what year did you complete the government service commitment for this award?

D2. How did you satisfy the government service requirement for this Boren Award?
- Repayment
- Other [Specify]: _____

D3. What led you to choose repayment over completing the requirement through a job in the federal government?
- Unable to find qualifying employment by NSEP service deadline
- Pursued employment in a field or position that did not fulfill the NSEP service requirement
- Employer offered to repay NSEP award balance
- Other life circumstances and/or other personal commitments

DL1. What is your native language?

DL2. In which languages (other than your native language) do you feel comfortable reading a news article? Please select from the list all that apply.[1]

DL3. In which languages (other than your native language) do you feel comfortable describing the plot of a movie? Please select all that apply.

A1. How did you learn about the Boren program? Check all that apply.
- Academic adviser or faculty member
- Boren Awards website (BorenAwards.org)
- National Security Education Program (NSEP) or Defense Language and National Security Education Office (DLNSEO) website
- Social media (e.g., Facebook, Instagram, Twitter, LinkedIn)
- Other internet website (other than social media)
- Other Boren Award recipient
- National Security Education Program (NSEP) or Boren outreach event
- National Youth Leadership Forum
- Other federal scholarship program (Critical Language Scholarship [CLS], STAR-TALK, etc.)
- Boren campus representative
- Other [Specify, but please do not include any personally identifying information in your response]:

A2. For what other scholarships, fellowships or awards did you apply, in addition to Boren? Check all that you **applied** for.
- I did not apply for any other scholarships, fellowships, or awards

---

[1] The survey presented a list of 72 languages, the option "none," and an option to select "other language, not listed" and provide the name of the language in a free response field.

- The Language Flagship (separate from the Boren program)
- Benjamin A. Gilman International Scholarship
- Charles B. Rangel International Affairs Graduate Fellowship
- Critical Language Scholarship (CLS)
- Department of State's Diplomacy Fellows Program
- Foreign Language and Area Studies program (FLAS)
- Freeman Award
- Fulbright-Hays Doctoral Dissertation Research Abroad Fellowship
- Fulbright Fellowship
- Graduate Assistance in Areas of National Need (GAANN)
- International Research and Exchanges Board (IREX)
- Jacob J. Javits Award
- National Security Language Initiative for Youth award
- National Science Foundation fellowship or grant
- Office of Personnel Management Presidential Management Fellowship (PMF)
- Social Science Research Council fellowship or grant
- Thomas R. Pickering Foreign Affairs Fellowship
- Mellon Fellowship
- University departmental/division grant
- Reserve Officers' Training Corps (ROTC) scholarship
- Other [Specify]: _____

A3.   What other scholarships, fellowships, or awards did you actually receive in addition to Boren? Check all that you **received**.
- I did not receive any other scholarships, fellowships, or awards
- The Language Flagship (separate from the Boren program)
- Benjamin A. Gilman International Scholarship
- Charles B. Rangel International Affairs Graduate Fellowship
- Critical Language Scholarship (CLS)
- Department of State's Diplomacy Fellows Program
- Foreign Language and Area Studies program (FLAS)
- Freeman Award
- Fulbright-Hays Doctoral Dissertation Research Abroad Fellowship
- Fulbright Fellowship
- Graduate Assistance in Areas of National Need (GAANN)
- International Research and Exchanges Board (IREX)
- Jacob J. Javits Award
- National Security Language Initiative for Youth award
- National Science Foundation fellowship or grant
- Office of Personnel Management Presidential Management Fellowship (PMF)
- Social Science Research Council fellowship or grant

- Thomas R. Pickering Foreign Affairs Fellowship
- Mellon Fellowship
- University departmental/division grant
- Reserve Officers' Training Corps (ROTC) scholarship
- Other [Specify: _____]

A4.   What other scholarships, fellowships, or awards did you actually complete in addition to Boren? Check all that you **completed**.
- I did not complete any other scholarships, fellowships, or awards
- The Language Flagship (separate from the Boren program)
- Benjamin A. Gilman International Scholarship
- Charles B. Rangel International Affairs Graduate Fellowship
- Critical Language Scholarship (CLS)
- Department of State's Diplomacy Fellows Program
- Foreign Language and Area Studies program (FLAS)
- Freeman Award
- Fulbright-Hays Doctoral Dissertation Research Abroad Fellowship
- Fulbright Fellowship
- Graduate Assistance in Areas of National Need (GAANN)
- International Research and Exchanges Board (IREX)
- Jacob J. Javits Award
- National Security Language Initiative for Youth award
- National Science Foundation fellowship or grant
- Office of Personnel Management Presidential Management Fellowship (PMF)
- Social Science Research Council fellowship or grant
- Thomas R. Pickering Foreign Affairs Fellowship
- Mellon Fellowship
- University departmental/division grant
- Reserve Officers' Training Corps (ROTC) scholarship
- Other [Specify]: _____

A5.   Earlier, you indicated that you applied for the Office of Personnel Management Presidential Management Fellowship (PMF). Did you use your PMF position to satisfy your Boren service-requirement position? (*Yes, No*)

A6.   Earlier, you indicated that you applied for the Department of State's Diplomacy Fellows Program. Did you subsequently enter the Foreign Service? (*Yes, No*)

We would like to know what attracted you to the Boren Awards program. Please rate the importance of each of these factors in your decision to apply to the Boren Awards program as *very important, somewhat important, somewhat unimportant,* or *very unimportant*.

A7. Interest in working in the federal government

A8. Opportunity for language study

A9. Opportunity for cultural learning

A10. Opportunity for regional study

A11. Opportunity for overseas experience

A12. Interest in funding and support

A13. Opportunity to be part of the Boren Scholars and Fellows network

A14. Possibility of receiving mentoring

A15. Opportunity to connect with my heritage/background

A16. Other [Specify, but please do not include any identifying information in your response:]

A17. Were you considering seeking employment with the Federal Government prior to learning about the Boren program? (*Yes, No*)

A18. How significant was your Boren experience in influencing your career path?
    – Very significant
    – Somewhat significant
    – Neither significant nor insignificant
    – Somewhat insignificant
    – Very insignificant

A19. Were you in the U.S. military, reserves, or participating in a Reserve Officers' Training Corps (ROTC) program at the time of your Boren Award? (*Yes, No, Not sure*)

In this section, you will be asked questions about your experiences and career path after your most recent Boren Award. These questions will include your postaward educational and professional experiences.

P1. Did you pursue any additional education following the completion of the degree you were working on at the time of your Boren Scholarship or Fellowship? (*Yes, No*)

P2. How many of each of these degrees or certificates have you ever begun, even if you did not complete it? Select 0 if you never pursued the degree or certificate.

P2.1 Ph.D. or other doctoral degree

P2.2 Master's degree

P2.3 J.D.

P2.4 M.B.A.

P2.5 Bachelor's degree

P2.6 Certificate

Please answer the following questions about your post-Boren employment. The information from these questions will be analyzed only in the aggregate, and not associated with any individual person.

P3.   How many jobs have you had since completing the degree associated with your Boren Scholarship or Fellowship, including the job that satisfied your Boren government service commitment? (*0, 1, 2, 3, 4 or more*)?

P4.1. What was the job title for your first job after completing the degree associated with your Boren Scholarship or Fellowship?

P5.1   In what year did you start this job?

P6.1. How would you categorize this job?
  – U.S. federal government (civilian employee)
  – Federal contractor
  – Educational institution
  – State government
  – Local government (city, county, school district)
  – U.S. military service, active duty, or Commissioned Corps government
  – For-profit company or organization other than federal contractor
  – Not-for-profit organization
  – FFRDC
  – Other [Specify]: _____

P7.1. For which federal agency did you work?

P8.1. What is your best estimate of your GS level when you began employment with this agency?

P9.1. If other pay scale (foreign service, NSPS), please specify pay grade.

P10.1. What is/was the name of the company where you were a federal contractor?

P11.1. For what federal agency is or was the contract? (If the contract was for more than one agency, please select the primary contracting agency.)

P12.1. What is the best estimate of your GS equivalent level when you entered employment with this company?

P13.1. Did you view your federal contractor position as a way to transition into a federal government position? (*Yes, No*)

P14.1. Are you still employed with this agency or company? (*Yes, No*)

P15.1. Did this position fulfill your Boren service requirement? (*Yes, No*)

[Each respondent who reported multiple jobs was presented with the same questions as in P4.1 through P15.1 for their second, third, and most recent jobs, respectively.]

PINTRO1. Your answers in the preceding questions indicate that you are still employed by the federal government.

P17.   What is your current GS level?

P18.   If other pay scale (Foreign Service, NSPS, etc.), please specify pay grade.

P19.   How long do you intend to stay with the federal government?
   – One year or less
   – Between 1 and 3 years
   – Between 3 and 5 years
   – Between 5 and 10 years
   – Entire career

PINTRO2. Your answers in the preceding question indicate that you are no longer employed by the federal government.

P20.   What is your best estimate of your GS level at the time you left employment with this agency?

P21.   If other pay scale (Foreign Service, NSPS, etc.), please specify pay grade.

P22.   Why did you leave employment with this agency? Check all that apply.
   – Not a good match for skills
   – Opportunity in another agency/employer
   – Change in career or professional interests
   – Went back to school
   – Job location/duty station
   – Position was an internship
   – Position was temporary (e.g., Schedule A(r) appointment)
   – Family related reasons (e.g., children, spouse's job moved)
   – Completed service requirement
   – Salary and benefits
   – Lack of career/promotion opportunities
   – Working conditions (e.g., hours, working environment)
   – Other [Specify, but please do not include any personally identifying information in your response]:

P23. In what year did you leave?

P24. While you were working in any of these positions, were you also waiting for an agency security clearance? (*Yes, No*)

P25. How long did the security clearance process take?
- Less than 1 year
- 1 year or more but less than 3 years
- 3 years or more but less than 5 years
- 5 years or more
- Did not finish clearance processing

The following section asks questions about the position you used to fulfill your service requirement. If you received more than one Boren Scholarship, or both a Boren Scholarship and Fellowship, please answer the remaining questions about your *most recent* award only.

S1. Did you use any of the following as a resource when applying for a full-time job after completing your degree? Check all that apply.
- NSEP office
- NSEP job board
- NSEP networking contacts
- Boren mentor or peer networks
- Boren alumni association
- Boren group on LinkedIn
- Boren group on Facebook
- Other [specify, but please do not include any identifying information in your response]:
- None

S2. Which factors weighed most heavily in your decision to accept the position that you used to fulfill your service commitment? Check all that apply.
- Good match for skill set
- Good match for topical interest
- Desire to work in that agency/employer or interest in specific position
- Need to fulfill the service commitment in the specified amount of time
- Compensation (salary and benefits)
- Career/promotion potential
- It was the only position offered
- Job location/duty station
- Other [specify, but please do not include any identifying information in your response]:

S3.   Were special hiring authorities (such as Schedule A, National Defense Authorization Act FY 10, National Defense Authorization Act FY 13) used to hire you to your service-requirement position? (*Yes, No, Don't know*)

S4.   Did you learn about this job through an NSEP exclusive job posting for Boren Scholars and Fellows? (*Yes, No, Don't know*)

To what extent do you agree with the following statements?

S5.   My Boren Scholarship/Fellowship experience helped me get my service-requirement position. (*Strongly agree, Agree, Neither agree nor disagree, Disagree, Strongly disagree*)

S6.   My Boren Scholarship/Fellowship experience helped me succeed in my service-requirement position. (*Strongly agree, Agree, Neither agree nor disagree, Disagree, Strongly disagree*)

S7.   What generalizable skills did you gain while completing your Boren Scholarship/Fellowship? Check all that apply.
      - Language proficiency
      - Regional proficiency
      - Cross-cultural understanding
      - Writing
      - Research
      - Problem solving
      - Strategic planning
      - Analytical thinking
      - Interpersonal communication
      - Ability to perform under pressure
      - Building project timetables
      - Monitoring progress against agreed upon goals
      - Confidence in adapting to new/unfamiliar settings
      - Professionalism
      - Didn't acquire generalizable skills during Boren
      - Other [specify, but please do not include any identifying information in your response]:

S8.   Which of these skills did you use in your service-requirement position? Check all that apply.
      - Language proficiency
      - Regional proficiency
      - Cross-cultural understanding

- Writing
- Research
- Problem solving
- Strategic planning
- Analytical thinking
- Interpersonal communication
- Ability to perform under pressure
- Building project timetables
- Monitoring progress against agreed upon goals
- Confidence in adapting to new/unfamiliar settings
- Professionalism
- Didn't use any of these skills in the service-requirement position
- Other [specify, but please do not include any identifying information in your response]:

S9. Are you still working in the position you used to fulfill your service requirement? (*Yes, No, Not applicable*)

This section asks questions about your current or most recent employment.

E1. Having a Boren Scholarship/Fellowship helped me to succeed in my current or most recent position. (*Strongly agree, Agree, Neither agree nor disagree, Disagree, Strongly disagree*)

E2. Having a Boren Scholarship/Fellowship helped me get my current or most recent position. (*Strongly agree, Agree, neither agree nor disagree, Disagree, strongly disagree*)

E3. What skills have you used in your most recent position, regardless of whether you gained them from Boren? Check all that apply.
- Language proficiency
- Regional proficiency
- Cross-cultural understanding
- Writing
- Research
- Problem solving
- Strategic planning
- Analytic thinking
- Interpersonal communication
- Ability to perform under pressure
- Building project timetables

- Monitoring progress against agreed upon goals
- Adapting to new/unfamiliar settings
- Professionalism
- Don't use skills acquired during Boren
- Other [specify, but please do not include any identifying information in your response]:
- None of the above/Not applicable

Please rate the importance of each of the following on your decision to accept your current or most recent position. (*Very important, Somewhat important, Slightly important, Not at all important*)

C1.   Benefits
C2.   Location
C3.   Work/life balance
C4.   Salary
C5.   Expected job satisfaction
C6.   Desire to work in a particular agency, institution, or company
C7.   Desire to work in a certain field
C8.   Match for your skills
C9.   Alignment with your topical interests
C10.   Alignment with your personal values
C11.   Ability to work with existing colleagues and professional network
C12.   Opportunity to expand your contacts and professional network
C13.   Learning opportunity
C14.   Advice from professional contacts or mentors
C15.   Advice from personal contacts
C16.   Quality or quantity of other job offers

Please rate how influential the skills and perspectives you gained from your Boren Award have been on your career path. (*Very influential, Somewhat influential, Slightly influential, Not influential, Not applicable*)

C17.   Skills acquired while overseas, such as language and regional proficiency
C18.   Increased awareness and commitment to U.S. national security
C19.   Increased awareness and commitment to international affairs
C20.   Self-assurance in position as a global citizen
C21.   Self-assurance in ability to be a consensus-builder and partner

Please rate how influential the resources you gained from your Boren Award have been on your career path. (*Very influential, Somewhat influential, Slightly influential, Not influential, Not applicable*)

C22. Networking opportunities
C23. Hiring authorities
C24. Boren Awards name recognition
C25. Prestige of the Boren Awards
C26. Access to the Boren Forum and/or NSEP Alumni Association
C27. Eligibility in the Department of State's Diplomacy Fellows Program
C28. Mentoring from Boren alumni

We are interested in your perceptions about how the Boren Award affected your academic studies and career opportunities. Please consider how influential your Boren Award was to each of the following. (*Very influential, Somewhat influential, Slightly influential, Not influential, Not applicable*)

C29. Pursuing my language study
C30. Achieving advanced language proficiency
C31. Traveling overseas for a language immersion/study abroad experience
C32. Receiving additional fellowship or awards
C33. Working in the federal government
C34. Working in the field in which I am currently employed
C35. Receiving the offer for my service-requirement position
C36. Receiving the offer for my current or most recent position

O1. Your opinion matters. Please share any additional thoughts below pertaining to your Boren Scholarship/Fellowship or the Boren Awards program in the box below. ***Please do not include any personally identifiable information in your response.***

_____

Thank you for completing this survey! We very much appreciate your input. If you have any questions, please contact us at BorenProject@rand.org.

Thank you for your interest in this study. Based on some of your answers, you are not currently eligible to participate. If you have any questions, please contact us at ask RAND@rand.org.

Abbreviations

AS	administration and support
CIA	Central Intelligence Agency
CLS	Critical Language Scholarship
DHS	Department of Homeland Security
DLNSEO	Defense Language and National Security Education Office
DoD	Department of Defense
DOS	Department of State
ES	Executive Service
FFRDC	federally funded research and development center
FLAS	Foreign Language and Area Studies
FY	fiscal year
GAANN	Graduate Assistance in Areas of National Need
GS	General Schedule
HR	Human Resources
IIE	Institute of International Education
IREX	International Research and Exchanges
KSAOs	knowledge, skills, ability, and other characteristics
NC	network and communications
NDAA	National Defense Authorization Act
NDAA'13	National Defense Authorization Act for Fiscal Year 2013
NDRI	National Defense Research Institute
NGO	nongovernmental organization
NSEA	National Security Education Act
NSEP	National Security Education Program
NSRD	National Security Research Division
OPM	Office of Personnel Management
PMF	Presidential Management Fellowship
PO	program options
ROI	return on investment
ROTC	Reserve Officers' Training Corps
USAID	U.S. Agency for International Development

Bibliography

Allen-Ebrahimian, Bethany, and Robbie Gramer, "State Department Suspends Yet Another Fellowship Program," *Foreign Policy*, July 19, 2017.

American Marketing Association, "About AMA: Definition of Marketing," July 2013. As of July 16, 2024:
https://www.ama.org/about-ama

Andersen, Lotte Bøgh, Ulrich Thy Jensen, and Anne Mette Kjeldsen, "Public Service Motivation and Its Implications for Public Service," in Helen Sullivan, Helen Dickinson, and Hayley Henderson, eds., *The Palgrave Handbook of the Public Servant*, Palgrave Macmillan, 2020.

Bhaimiya, Sawdah, "Gen Z Expect to Change Careers 3 Times throughout Their Lives—Once More than Any Other Generation: Survey," Business Insider, November 3, 2023. As of January 5, 2024:
https://www.businessinsider.com/gen-z-like-to-job-hop-change-career-survey-2023-11

Boren Awards, homepage, undated-a. As of December 14, 2023:
https://www.borenawards.org

Boren Awards, "Essays—National Security & Careers in Public Service: Essay 2—Motivation & Public Service Careers," webpage, undated-b. As of December 14, 2023:
https://www.borenawards.org/essays#public-service

Boren Awards, "Selecting an Eligible Study Program," webpage, undated-c. As of December 14, 2023:
https://www.borenawards.org/eligible-programs

Bright, Leonard, "Government Career Interests, Perceptions of Fit, and Degree Orientations: Exploring Their Relationship in Public Administration Graduate Programs," *Teaching Public Administration*, Vol. 36, No. 1, 2018.

Bright, Leonard, and Cole Blease Graham, Jr., "Why Does Interest in Government Careers Decline Among Public Affairs Graduate Students?" *Journal of Public Affairs Education*, Vol. 21, No. 4, 2015.

Bright, Leonard, "Government Career Interests, Perceptions of Fit, and Degree Orientations: Exploring Their Relationship in Public Administration Graduate Programs," *Teaching Public Administration*, Vol. 36, No. 1, 2018.

Defense Language and National Security Education Office, "Boren Awards," webpage, undated-a. As of December 14, 2023:
https://dlnseo.org/Programs/NSEP/Boren

Defense Language and National Security Education Office, *Celebrating 30 Years: 1991–2021*, undated-b. As of December 14, 2023:
https://dlnseo.org/sites/default/files/DLNSEO%20NSEP%2030th%20book23_web.pdf

Defense Language and National Security Education Office, "NSEP Annual Reports," webpage, undated-c. As of December 14, 2023:
https://dlnseo.org/Publications

Defense Language and National Security Education Office, *2023 Annual Report: National Security Education Program*, C-62DBC45, December 18, 2023. As of February 26, 2024:
https://dlnseo.org/sites/default/files/2023%20NSEP%20Annual%20Report.pdf

Deloitte, *2023 Gen Z and Millennial Survey*, 2023. As of December 12, 2024:
https://www2.deloitte.com/content/dam/Deloitte/si/Documents/deloitte-2023-genz-millennial
-survey.pdf

Department of Defense Instruction 1025.02, *National Security Education Program (NSEP) and NSEP Service Agreement*, U.S. Department of Defense, January 3, 2017.

DLNSEO—*See* Defense Language and National Security Education Office.

Doubleday, Justin, "Why Some Security Clearance Cases Are Taking Longer in Recent Months," *Federal News Network*, November 24, 2023.

Doverspike, Dennis, Lei Qin, Marc Porter Magee, Andrea Snell, and Pamela Vaiana, "The Public Sector as a Career Choice: Antecedents of an Expressed Interest in Working for the Federal Government," *Public Personnel Management*, Vol. 40, No. 2, 2011.

Ertas, Nevbahar, "Turnover Intentions and Work Motivations of Millennial Employees in Federal Service," *Public Personnel Management*, Vol. 44, No. 3, 2015.

Executive Order 13583, "Establishing a Coordinated Government-Wide Initiative to Promote Diversity and Inclusion in the Federal Workforce," Executive Office of the President, August 18, 2011.

Homberg, Fabian, Dermot McCarthy, and Vurain Tabvuma, "A Meta-Analysis of the Relationship Between Public Service Motivation and Job Satisfaction," *Public Administration Review*, Vol. 75, No. 5, 2015.

Jones, Yvonne D., *Disability Employment: Hiring Has Increased but Actions Needed to Assess Retention, Training, and Reasonable Accommodation Efforts: Report to the Committee on Oversight and Reform, U.S. House of Representatives*, U.S. Government Accountability Office, GAO-20-384, June 2020.

McGinn, Gail H., "Government Needs and Shortages in Foreign Language and Regional Expertise and Knowledge," paper presented at Internationalization of U.S. Education in the Twenty-First Century: The Future of International and Foreign Language Studies, conference, College of William & Mary, 2014.

McKinsey, *Diversity Matters Even More*, McKinsey & Company, 2023.

National Commission on Military, National, and Public Service, *Inspired to Serve: The Final Report of the National Commission on Military, National, and Public Service*, March 2020.

National Security Education Program, homepage, undated-a. As of June 21, 2024:
https://www.nsepnet.org/Default.aspx

National Security Education Program, "Advice & Resources," webpage, undated-b. As of June 21, 2024:
https://www.nsepnet.org/tips.aspx

National Security Education Program, "NSEP Job Board," undated-d. As of December 14, 2023:
https://www.nsepnet.org/JobBoard.aspx

Ng, Eddy, and Jasmine McGinnis Johnson, "Game of Loans: The Relationship Between Education Debt, Social Responsibility Concerns, and Making a Career Choice in the Public, Private, and Nonprofit Sectors," *Nonprofit and Voluntary Sector Quarterly*, Vol. 49, No. 2, 2020.

NSEP—*See* National Security Education Program.

OPM—*See* U.S. Office of Personnel Management.

Oxford Dictionaries Online. "New Oxford American Dictionary," third edition. Oxford University Press.

Partnership for Public Service/National Association of Colleges and Employers, "Federal Leaders Face Challenges Attracting Top College Graduates to Government Service," issue brief, February 2012. As of December 14, 2023:
https://ourpublicservice.org/wp-content/uploads/2018/09/federa-leaders-face-challenges.pdf

Partnership for Public Service/National Association of Colleges and Employers, "College Students Are Attracted to Federal Service, but Agencies Need to Capitalize on Their Interest," issue brief, March 2014. As of October 20, 2023:
https://ourpublicservice.org/wp-content/uploads/2014/03/08cfe7a90149145f2e0f90a564ae1402 -1396883817.pdf

Pew Research Center, *Early Benchmarks Show "Post-Millennials" on Track to Be Most Diverse, Best-Educated Generation Yet*, November 2018. As of May 18, 2023:
https://www.pewresearch.org/social-trends/wp-content/uploads/sites/3/2018/11/Post-Millennials -Report_final-11.13pm.pdf

Public Law 102-183, Intelligence Authorization Act, Fiscal Year 1992, December 4, 1991.

Public Law 111-84, National Defense Authorization Act for Fiscal Year 2010, October 28, 2009.

Rose, Roger P., "Preferences for Careers in Public Work: Examining the Government-Nonprofit Divide Among Undergraduates Through Public Service Motivation," *American Review of Public Administration*, Vol. 43, No. 4, 2012.

Santinha, Gonçalo, Teresa Carvalho, Teresa Forte, Alexandre Fernandes, and Jéssica Tavares, "Profiling Public Sector Choice: Perceptions and Motivational Determinants at the Pre-Entry Level," *Sustainability*, Vol. 13, No. 3, 2021.

Schroth, Holly, "Are You Ready for Gen Z in the Workplace?" *California Management Review*, Vol. 61, No. 3, 2019

Simon, Paul, *The Tongue-Tied American: Confronting The Foreign Language Crisis.* New York: Continuum, 1980.

Twenge, J. M., *iGen: Why Today's Super-Connected Kids Are Growing up Less Rebellious, More Tolerant, Less Happy, and Completely Unprepared for Adulthood.* Atria Books, 2017.

USAJOBS, homepage, undated. As of June 23, 2024:
https://www.usajobs.gov

U.S. Office of Personnel Management, "Diversity, Equity, Inclusion, and Accessibility," webpage, undated-a. As of April 2, 2024:
https://www.opm.gov/policy-data-oversight/diversity-equity-inclusion-and-accessibility/

U.S. Office of Personnel Management, *Promising Practices for Diversity, Equity, Inclusion, and Accessibility in the Federal Workforce*, undated-b. As of April 2, 2024:
https://www.opm.gov/policy-data-oversight/diversity-equity-inclusion-and-accessibility/promising -practices-for-diversity-equity-inclusion-and-accessibility-in-the-federal-workforce.pdf

Viechnicki, Peter, *Understanding Millennials in Government: Debunking Myths About Our Youngest Public Servants*, Deloitte University Press, 2015. As of December 14, 2023:
https://www2.deloitte.com/content/dam/insights/us/articles/millennials-in-government-federal -workforce/DUP-1450_Millennials-in-govt_vFINAL_12.2.15.pdf

White House, "Executive Order on Diversity, Equity, Inclusion, and Accessibility in the Federal Workforce," brief, June 25, 2021a. As of April 4, 2024:
https://www.whitehouse.gov/briefing-room/presidential-actions/2021/06/25/executive-order-on -diversity-equity-inclusion-and-accessibility-in-the-federal-workforce/

White House, *Government-Wide Strategic Plan to Advance Diversity, Equity, Inclusion, and Accessibility in the Federal Workforce*, November 2021b. As of April 4, 2024:
https://www.whitehouse.gov/wp-content/uploads/2021/11/Strategic-Plan-to-Advance-Diversity
-Equity-Inclusion-and-Accessibility-in-the-Federal-Workforce-11.23.21.pdf

White House, "*Strengthening the Federal Workforce*, 2022. As of December 14, 2023:
https://www.whitehouse.gov/wp-content/uploads/2021/05/ap_5_strengthening_fy22.pdf

Wolfanger, Jessica, S., Sarah M. Russell, and Zachary T. Miller, *Boren Scholarship and Fellowship Survey*, CNA, October 2014. As of December 14, 2023:
https://www.cna.org/archive/CNA_Files/pdf/drm-2014-u-007929-final.pdf